HISTORY AND VALUE

HISTORY
AND
VALUE

The Clarendon Lectures and
the Northcliffe Lectures
1987

FRANK KERMODE

CLARENDON PRESS · OXFORD

*This book has been printed digitally and produced in a standard specification
in order to ensure its continuing availability*

OXFORD
UNIVERSITY PRESS

Great Clarendon Street, Oxford OX2 6DP

Oxford University Press is a department of the University of Oxford.
It furthers the University's objective of excellence in research, scholarship,
and education by publishing worldwide in

Oxford New York

Auckland Bangkok Buenos Aires Cape Town Chennai
Dar es Salaam Delhi Hong Kong Istanbul Karachi Kolkata
Kuala Lumpur Madrid Melbourne Mexico City Mumbai Nairobi
São Paulo Shanghai Singapore Taipei Tokyo Toronto

Oxford is a registered trade mark of Oxford University Press
in the UK and in certain other countries

Published in the United States
by Oxford University Press Inc., New York

ISBN 0-19-812224-1

To Anita

PREFACE

THIS book is the consequence of two invitations: from the Oxford University Press and the Oxford Faculty of English to give the Clarendon Lectures, and from University College, London, to give the Northcliffe Lectures. The Oxford lectures were the first of the name, the London lectures the latest in a long and distinguished series. It seemed a good idea to combine them in one book; I only wish it could convey some of the pleasures incident to the delivery of the lectures, but the satisfactions of Oxford even in dark January, and of Gower Street—more familiar but no less valued—even in cold February are not negotiable in print.

I should here say a word about the relation between the two series, now the two parts of this book. Asked to give two sets of lectures, I had an idea for each, and was sure that I should find a connection between them. The Clarendon series was to say something about the literature of the Thirties, which happened to be the modern literature of my own youth; I was twenty when the decade ended. Since I expected to be addressing an audience consisting largely of people who were about twenty when they came, almost half a century later, to the lectures—people to whom the 1930s were in effect about as remote as the 1830s—I resolved to be explicit about a good many things which, though their elders might think them commonplace, the young wouldn't know and might yet be interested to hear about. For the same reason I wanted to establish my own aged credentials by letting it be known that I had actually been around at the time; hence an element of anecdote which I hope will not be taken for anecdotage. It is an advantage of sorts to have had some acquaintance at first hand with what is now a historical context, to be studied mostly in books and probably reduced to convenient but potentially misleading formulas. Moreover, for reasons related to the general question of literary survival, I needed to talk about a number of books well thought of in my day and now more or less forgotten, though not by me and possibly a few others.

The Northcliffe series was to be more generally on the topics of literary evaluation and permanence and the various distortions of historical context. The link, which I tried to make firmer by echoing in the opening lecture of the second series some of the themes of the first, was my use of the Thirties as a testing ground for questions of survival, and assumptions about historical periods. There was also the difficult question of value, or of valuation; and the idea that books can die from ignorance, our ignorance, even if they seem to have qualities—the boldness to transgress, to break moulds and conventions—that by hindsight we may think to be indications of inherent value.

Among my audience at Oxford there were those, more widely read than I, who were able to remind or tell me of other books about men in love with, or anyway interested in, young girls. They include Henry James's *Watch and Ward*, Sean Webster's *Daddy-Long-Legs*, which Barbara Everett describes as 'a more girlish *Watch and Ward*', and Rosamund Bland's *The Man in the Stone House*. I am grateful to my informants, and also to Mr Stephen Haggard, for telling me more about his grandfather, the author of *Nya*. I have resisted the temptation to squeeze all this information into the opening lecture, fearing for such balance as it has.

I am most grateful to Professor John Carey, the Merton Professor, who found time in a hectically busy life to see that my time in Oxford was comfortable and pleasant; and to the Warden and Fellows of Merton, for two weeks my courteous hosts. My old friends John and Eirian Wain were more than hospitable. To Kim Scott Walwyn of Oxford University Press I am grateful for attentions through the whole process from invitation to book. In Bloomsbury I was pampered by the Provost of University College, Sir James Lighthill, and by Professor Karl Miller and his colleagues in the English Department. Once again, it seems unreasonable to have had such a good time while engaged in the normally quite painful process of writing a book. There *were* pains earlier on, caused partly by the rigour with which the dedicatee criticized earlier drafts. For that indispensable service I am, as so often before, greatly indebted to her.

F. K.
Cambridge
April 1987

CONTENTS

PART ONE

Bourgeois Literature in the Thirties

1 · Bourgeois Literature in the Thirties

THE word 'bourgeois' in the title may look a bit odd, but I think it is accurate. Most of our literature is bourgeois without our feeling we need to keep on calling it that, but the Thirties was a brief period during which politics so polarized books and their writers— demanded so close an attention to questions of class—that one can hardly discuss that bit of literary history without frequent use of the term and its partner 'proletarian'.

To many people it seems self-evident that too naked an interest in such matters is bad for literature. They might want to say that books don't become important simply because they are about issues that are held to be important outside books; they deny that books may be good because they favour good causes and bad because they don't. They find it easy to distinguish between literature and propaganda, to cherish the one and discard the other.

And anyway, there are unmanageably many books, and most of them have to be ignored; so tests of this sort, however approximate, have a practical value as weed-killers. We use them, along with other excuses and myths, to protect the chosen plants. How we do these things, and what the consequences of our doing them may be, are the sorts of topic I mean to address in this book.

It is surprising, when you come to think of it, that in an age often described as sceptical, an age of criticism, post-criticism, etc., we speak so rarely of our reasons for choosing to speak regularly of x and hardly ever of y. Unless we have some political end in view (substituting another set of unexamined prejudices for the one already in place) we are inclined to leave the entire business of judgement to that old common arbitrator, Time.

Looking around for some instances of our readiness to do so, I found I hardly needed to stir from the breakfast table. Here is Anthony Burgess, on 14 November 1986, telling us that 'only the future can decide who is as good as, or not inferior to, William Golding'.[1] On the same day I came across Barbara Everett's *obiter dictum*: 'Most great writers manage to survive, in one way or

---

[1] *Times Literary Supplement*, 14 Nov. 1986.

another.'[2] We say such things without considering that they are meaningless unless we are prepared to name some great writers who haven't survived, and explain why they are great notwithstanding. The habit is not confined to literary critics: on 3 October 1986 I find Norbert Lynton remarking, also in the *Times Literary Supplement*, that 'Kokoschka was an energetic painter and an outstanding draughtsman. In time we shall know whether he was a truly great artist.'[3] Time will tell—some, like Dr Johnson, think in a hundred years, some in fifty, and some, like Cyril Connolly, in ten—what is good or great, and do so without specifiable human intervention.

Robert Graves, who showed in his Clark Lectures and elsewhere that he thought he could perform the work of Time on his contemporaries, once wondered why other critics were so timid about making judgements:

> Any honest housewife would sort them out,
> Having a nose for fish, an eye for apples.
> Is it any mystery who are the sound,
> And who the rotten? Never, by her lights.
>
> Any honest housewife who, by ill-fortune,
> Ever engaged a slut to scrub for her
> Could instantly distinguish from the workers
> The lazy, the liars and the petty thieves.
>
> Does this denote a peculiar sixth sense
> Gifted to housewives for their vestal needs?
> Or is it a failure of the usual five
> In all unthrifty writers on this head?[4]

As a matter of fact we are always, in unofficial ordinary conversation, doing what this housewife does—sorting out the sound and the rotten, confidently anticipating the action of time. It is when we become critics that the whole thing comes to be problematic to the extent that we shirk judgements altogether. In some of the highest critical circles there has been for quite some time a tendency to avoid all questions of value. Indeed a recent article by Barbara Herrnstein Smith, called 'Contingencies of Value', says that 'literary evaluation' has been 'evaded and explicitly exiled' by 'the literary academy'.[5] Nobody could accuse Northrop Frye of evading it, but he does

[2] *Poets in their Time* (1986), p. 32.   [3] p. 1086.
[4] *Collected Poems* (1959), p. 137.   [5] In R. von Hallberg (ed.), *Canons* (1984), 5.

explicitly exile it, and he was only the most influential of the transatlantic value-free critics. Over here of course Dr Leavis was, on the contrary, strenuous in evaluation and revaluation. And now these activities are in favour again, not in consequence of Dr Leavis's advocacy but because many people are for many reasons asking questions about the power of institutions over the culture in general, for example over university syllabuses and more generally over the list of things seekers of literary valuables ought to read. I am thinking of the critique of institutionalized values, ever more urgent, that we now hear from feminists and from racial minorities who suspect that the choices of an élite are not made in their interests, and that the existing canons are the production neither of time nor of infallible taste.

These assaults, as I say, are on the institution rather than on its choice of books, but they do serve to reintroduce the question of literary valuation, and that is my topic. For the moment, however, I shall operate within the limited area I named at the outset, namely Thirties literature. One reason for choosing this period was a personal one which may not be of very high interest: it is that in the last half of that decade I was old enough to read books as they appeared, and some I shall discuss I have reread after an interval of half a century, I hope with the benefit of binocular vision, but at all events with the advantage of hindsight. Much that gave immediate pleasure in those years (as in any other years) is now forgotten or reduced to a sort of archival half-life. Much that is not forgotten is thought little of. I believe some of the literature of the period has been treated unjustly by Time, by which I really mean us, prejudiced and indolent as we always are in these affairs.

There are myths about all periods (periods *are* myths) and we use them as formulas, as algorithms to programme the past and make it manageable. I'll return to that point later on. For the moment it's enough to say that the Thirties myth goes something like this: some writers of the time—some of the best writers of the time—were induced by its unfamiliar political pressures to write against their own bents. Uneasily allured by Communism, they professed a fatal interest in unemployment, the Spanish Civil War, the death throes of capitalism, the imminence of revolution and of world conflict. George Orwell, whose influence grew so enormously in the post-war years, had a lot to do with the establishment of this version, but some of the writers themselves also fostered it. Later they looked back and said that in those days they had been out of their depth, writing about matters they did not understand, half in love with a proletariat they knew nothing about. Quite soon they saw it wouldn't do, left the Party if they had joined it, retreated to Devon or the United States, and expressed shame at their immature follies. And this is the version now commonly accepted, here reported with only a slight degree of caricature as the truth (except for a few stubborn left-wingers) about the Thirties.

I shall try to offer an alternative myth, in which what that myth calls vices may appear as virtues; in which the literature the common myth condescends to is treated as valuable, and valuable to us, fifty years on. To some of them, it appeared that to stand aside and carry on as if nothing in the world concerned them except their own work, narrowly considered, would cause an injury not only to conscience but to such gifts as they felt they had. And we can't simply dismiss this view as mistaken, even if they themselves came to feel that it was.

Later I shall be discussing writers whom we don't mind calling major, usually having in mind their later achievements. But I begin by talking about a book almost certainly unread by anybody in this company except myself. I want to ask how it came about that this ostensibly serious book was condemned to neglect, but also to point out some of the differences between its silent condemnation and the condemnation by critical myth of other work which we cannot so easily afford to lose. I will take a minute to explain how I came to read it in the first place, and why I have read it again of late.

In June 1943 I was on board a French liner, the *Pasteur*, bound for New York. As I remember, I was the only passenger, for the main purpose of the voyage was not to take people to the United States but to collect thousands of American soldiers and deliver them to England. At that stage in the war the role of these big ships had become very specialized; they carried huge numbers of men in conditions of extreme discomfort, dispensing with escorts and successfully relying on speed and zigzag courses as their protection against submarines. For obvious reasons all peacetime luxuries had disappeared. Knowing this in advance I had with me what should have been a supply of reading large enough for the voyage; there would be no library. But then something happened I hadn't allowed for—the ship's main engine broke down, and for some considerable time we simply wallowed about in mid-Atlantic. The onset of that worst wartime fear, the fear of having nothing to read, was immediate. But rooting around the enormous ship I discovered, in some remote saloon, a little shelf of books. Randomly accumulated, they had no relation to the tastes and needs of rich Frenchmen before the war; they were more like the little heaps of abandoned novels you find in weekend cottages. There was nothing I really wanted to read, but I had to have something, and so bore off the longest novel on the shelf, which happened to be by an author I had heard of, though I hadn't known he was a novelist.

The novel was called *Nya*. I must have been rather taken with it; it stayed in my mind and over the next forty years (though it seems I wasn't quite interested enough to dig out a copy) I would sometimes mention it in the hope of finding somebody else who had read it. The only person I ever met who knew the book turned out to be the author's grandson. It was not until 1986 that I bestirred myself and found a copy. At first I merely wanted to know what it was about the book that had pleased me in my youth. Then it occurred to me that I could use it for the purposes of the present investigation.

Nya is about a love-affair between a man in his middle twenties, only a little older than I was when I first read the book, and a thirteen-year-old girl. It was published in 1938, a date at which the public, it may be useful to recall, was forbidden to read a novel about an affair between a lady and her gamekeeper. You might think, then, that a novel on such a subject would have caused a bit of a stir. But there seems to have been no outcry. Frank Morley accepted the novel for Faber and Faber without recorded misgivings, and the Chairman of the firm, Sir Geoffrey Faber, hardly a man to brook impropriety, was quite enthusiastic; he was kind to the author and urged him to write another novel at once, preferably in the manner of John Buchan.[6] L. P. Hartley, reviewing the book, remarked that it 'dealt with a new subject for a novel'; and another reviewer said that *Nya* had 'a theme before which even an experienced novelist might quail', but called the work 'fine and sensitive'.[7] And we shall see, I think, that one of the interesting things about *Nya* is just this: despite its subject it provided the censors, whether judicial or journalistic, with

[6] I am grateful to Faber and Faber for allowing me to read the relevant correspondence in their archives.

[7] Reviews quoted on the dust-jacket of the second edition, published in 1938, a month after the first.

no occasion for prosecution or public displays of indignation, though there was certainly no shortage of such watchdogs at the time.

At the start of the book the girl is with her family in Nyasaland, where her father is an overworked colonial officer. She is a child of nature, swift of foot as the leopard after which she is named. However, her mother and brother die of blackwater fever, as so many white people did in colonial Africa, and her father decides she must return to England; he has too much to do as it is, administering justice in 'God-forsaken Nyasaland', without taking care of a young girl. In England, he muses, 'no possible harm could befall her', so she is entrusted to the care of an uncle and aunt, and sent to boarding school.

Since she has been brought up to be a child of nature, Nya is not altogether well equipped for civilized society; she has never had any dealings with money, religion, and other important aspects of urban life. In some respects, however, she is more mature than her English contemporaries. On the boat home she flirts innocently with a young ship's officer, who chases her playfully round the deck and tells her she is 'more natural than the girls you'll meet at school'. Settled in Dorset, she misses her father and writes to him what are virtually love-letters. She dislikes England, not only because her father isn't there, but because the country seems to be 'organized entirely in favour of grown-up people', an arrangement she regards as justifying a certain amount of deceitfulness on her part.

Her uncle's household is well-to-do middle class of the period, with two indoor servants and a gardener. The uncle himself spends most of his time sitting in his study with *The Times*, smoking his pipe and keeping out of trouble. The aunt is a much stronger character; deploring Nya's education so far, she decides to give the girl 'an English training'. She interferes in Nya's choice of clothes (clothes are an important motif) and in her choice of friends, for the girl has struck up an acquaintance with some 'street-boys' and cannot yet understand why she must not do so. There is a polite struggle between natural and convention-encrusted morality. The aunt has a perpetual and to Nya inexplicable passion for 'talking things over'; the girl thinks that 'either it was right to do a thing or it was wrong', and no discussion is needed.

Nya's natural education has not taught her everything about nature, either, and she is surprised and shocked by her first period, which happens at school. Although she is there reassured and instructed, she understands that this is a matter she could not discuss with her father, even if he were at hand. Four hundred pages later she reflects that 'the whole trouble had begun then. And yet "trouble" wasn't quite the right word . . .'

The proximate cause of the 'trouble' is a young yachtsman whom she bumps into on the pier at Poole, breaking his pipe. (Nya, or the book she is in, seems to associate pipe-smoking with males of the right sort.) Young Simon reminds her of her father, and at first she thinks her feeling for him is a kind of homesickness. She dreams a lot, and now dreams of Simon—a flying dream of the sort arising, according to Freud in his study of Leonardo, from 'a longing to be capable of sexual performance'.[8] There might be some dispute as to whether the author was here tacitly referring to Freud, or unwittingly providing evidence for the plausibility of his observation. But the interesting and distinctive feature of Nya's dream is that, flying over Poole Harbour, she has to make her course conform to the marked channels and not overfly the shoals, exactly as if she were sailing. Allegorically this presumably means that sexual desire, however insistent, must be kept within rule. Her flight takes her to Simon's yacht, which, in the dream, is manned by her father. I think this curious scene was part of what ensured the book's survival in my memory.

Poole Harbour, I should add, is rather exactly described, and the author unsuccessfully asked his publisher to use the appropriate Admiralty chart on the jacket. One feature of the harbour is Brownsea Island, formerly inhabited but now deserted, which comes, in Nya's imagination, to represent an island of the dead. This fantasy was perhaps prompted by the affinity between the word 'Brownsea' and the word 'blackwater', the name of the disease which killed her mother and brother. She has a daydream in which she is aboard Simon's yacht, anchored off Brownsea Island; in this dream she is wearing the young man's sweater and shorts. Later on she actually does these things; fantasies of androgyny and death coalesce in a girl's dream, and then in the 'real' story.

Until Aunt Ethel finds out what is going on there is no voice in the novel to suggest that it is in any way reprehensible. 'Her instinct was

---

[8] *The Standard Edition of the Complete Psychological Works of Sigmund Freud*, trans. J. Strachey *et al.* (1953–64), xi. 125–6.

at work; one term of school in England hadn't been enough to destroy it;' Nya hadn't yet succumbed to civilization and its discontents. But the free play of instinct may be painful, and the onset of love is accompanied by a pain in the stomach. (I discovered later that this author quite often associates love with physical discomfort.) Stomach pain is not the only physiological disturbance caused by love; at their second meeting Simon observes the 'hot fervour' of Nya's glance. Here was something else she could not have told her father about, and the image of the young man is now rapidly dissociated from that of the father.

Simon, at this time, is puzzled about what is happening. Why is he spending so much time with Nya? He decides that it is because of his dislike for adult women, that the main reason why he likes Nya is that she is not 'full grown'. To be 'under age' is itself a desirable quality, for one is exempt from adult responsibilities. When Nya complains about oppressive grown-ups he advises her to resist; unlike him, he says, she has nothing to lose, she cannot be 'sacked, or put into prison'. Although Nya knows very well that she could suffer the juvenile equivalents of these sanctions, she agrees with him; and now the book more and more takes on the aspect of daydream, of a prepubescent, innocent liberty, a lost dormancy. It can hardly avoid hints of a different and more licentious subtext, but it gives the reader little encouragement to seek it out. Despite their physical maturity (Simon is twenty-six, and girls are said to mature early in Africa), the young people are represented as genuinely innocent, and the progress of their intimacy is slow and unpremeditated. Nya looks at her naked image in a mirror and finds it funny; but then she falls to thinking of the mystery of marriage, involuntarily associating nakedness and marriage with Simon, with sailing, and also with death. Taken by her uncle and aunt to see a film called *Desire*, she at once associates the word with sailing. Eventually Nya and Simon spend a night together on the yacht, are happy, are lovers, but without physical contact. Simon tells Nya to 'trust her instincts', but knows that he, not being under age and free, must 'hold back'. It is only when they are reunited after a separation of three weeks that they so much as kiss.

'Holding back' is for Simon a requirement of fear as well as of decency; he has no sexual experience. And it doesn't seem to occur to him that he really could go to prison if he didn't 'hold back'. Moreover he has a strong sense of propriety. Nya is much more dangerous, mature but wild. She is also rather like a boy, which contributes to the ambiguous innocence of the story. We are often warned off wrong interpretations, as when Nya finds among Simon's belongings on the yacht a cheap romance about a man kissing a sixteen-year-old girl, who supposes that the kiss was tantamount to a proposal of marriage. This romance used expressions such as 'flaming passion' and 'hot blood', and Nya, though she does not understand them, remembers that her father had always taught her to follow the counsel of George Bernard Shaw and avoid clichés, guessing correctly that the language of romance contained examples of these. Thus Nya is credited with the linguistic purity proper to her natural innocence; and at the same time a firm distinction is drawn between this novel and trashy romance. We note that Nya is several years the junior of the foolish and tawdry girl in the other story; she is still on the boundary of sexual maturity, still as much a child as a woman, still, in a way, a possible boy.

Most of the story is told from Nya's point of view, which licenses a certain *naïveté* in the tone, especially in the representation of Simon. A sportsman, an ocean-going yachtsman, he values Nya first as a friend, and as a non-woman. His dislike of grown women is not diminished by his forced acquaintance with Aunt Ethel, who, for all her bridge and tennis and good intentions, has obviously come close to unmanning her husband, and keenly wishes to denaturalize Nya and make her a lady. She seems to represent a class adapted over several generations to colonial administration, happy with tedious routine and with the comforts due to position, expressing its self-respect in a distrust of the poor amounting almost to hatred, and its social isolation in the brainwashing of its children. Yet in some ways she is presented as a worthy woman, and, although the novel sometimes seems on the point of making these criticisms explicit, it never quite does so. Nya herself comes to assume the rightness of such class-divisions and the desirability of formal or gentle manners; she abandons the street-boys and falls in love with a rich family and its clever children, Chinese pots, Classical music, and high civility levels.

At the end of the book Simon sails off in his yacht, accompanied by a trusty longshoreman who has been useful to him in his dealings with Nya. He is prepared to wait for her, to pass the time in voyaging across the Atlantic with a deferential member of the proletariat.

Of course the book doesn't put it like that. It is a long, slow, and apparently serious work. It appeared in the year of the Anschluss and of Munich, near the end of a decade of war and depression, an intensely political decade in which relations of class, and the attitudes of writers to class, were rapidly and, as it seemed, irrevocably changing. Not every novel has to take direct account of such matters. Nor need it be asked to consider possible endings, less benign, of the affair it describes. When it is discovered that he has spent a night with Nya, Simon has what might have been an awkward interview with Nya's uncle. He explains that Nya is the only woman he can talk to; the uncle is surprised to hear his niece described as a woman, but refrains from raising the question as to whether Simon had that night 'harmed' the girl. It is brutal Aunt Ethel, always wanting to have things out, who threatens to bring in a doctor to examine Nya; the girl doesn't understand why, but in fact the doctor never comes, and so this bit of forensic realism seems to be there only to discredit the conventional response of the older woman.

Perhaps I enjoyed this book in 1943 because it was in an odd way comforting; it suggested that you could fly and yet not depart from the channels, from the Admiralty chart; it proposed a pact between nature and culture. Its comments on English middle-class education and domestic life (of which I knew very little) were too mild to be disconcerting, and, if they masked a fear of women—middle-class women who unman their sedentary husbands—and a deep wish that girls should be as far as possible boys, I quite failed to make the right interpretation. I was doubtless imperceptive; but it should be re-membered that great changes have overtaken social and sexual relations in the past half-century, and the social and sexual assump-tions of *Nya* were much less surprising then than now, when they can seem as strange as those of a Renaissance court.

Obviously an inability to approve of its ideology need not prevent one from assigning a high value to books and poems. We assume without much question that under the unacceptable ideological surface there can be what Empsom calls 'permanent truths'.[9] But what are the qualities that ensure the availability of the work for our late approval on such grounds? We might, by way of answer, compare *Nya* with other books already admired, measuring its erotic

[9] *Some Versions of Pastoral* (1935), 4–5.

effect against the chiaroscuro of sexual representations in Ford
Madox Ford, or its handling of social relations with that of Henry
Green. By such means we might get a rough measure of what is
lacking in *Nya*; we might vaguely call it resonance, the resonance
afforded by the historical perspectives of Ford or by Green's rich
dialogue and the bold delicacy of his prose. Or we might compare
the book with others that treat of schools, servants, women, and
children. For surely there are names for the qualities that prevail, that
defy our habitually careless attitude to the past and to patterns of life
and thought as they existed before we saw through them. And
whatever they are, it seems on the evidence that *Nya*, like most other
novels, hasn't got them.

Nya was the first novel of an actor, Stephen Haggard. R A D A had
declared him 'unsusceptible to technique', but by 1938, when his
book appeared, he was already well known in the theatre. He won
the patronage of Athene Seyler, played Marchbanks in *Candida* with
Ann Harding and later with Diana Wynyard. His director thought
him 'too intense and intellectual' for the part, but Shaw praised his
performance. He played Chatterton in one piece and Gaudier-
Brzeska in another. He was Silvius in *As You Like It*, and made his
last and most celebrated stage appearance in Granville Barker's Old
Vic. *King Lear* in the early months of the war. As the Fool to
Gielgud's King he was quite unlike the grim old men we nowadays
see in the part; James Agate declared that he gave the role 'a
"silliness" of mind which was entirely beautiful'. 'Silly' sounds
right, a Cambridge–Bloomsbury word, with a flavour of election,
even of secular saintliness.

Despite these theatrical successes Haggard wanted to be a writer
rather than an actor, and it would be a mistake to underestimate the
strength of this resolve. He was greatly admired in the theatre, where
his success seemed assured, and his distinguished contemporaries
still remember him with great affection and respect.[10] He showed
little sign of being aware of what was going on in the big world,
which is perhaps not surprising—his friend, the equally successful
Peggy Ashcroft, was at this time asked what she thought of the

---

[10] Since this lecture was delivered I have heard Sir John Gielgud speak of Haggard
with unreserved admiration, not only as an actor but also as a man of high intelligence
and extraordinary personal charm. Sir John did not know *Nya*, or had perhaps
forgotten it.

slump, and answered 'What slump?'[11] Professional success, and London, cut him off from hunger, purges, and deathcamps. However, the war changed all that, for him as for so many others. He joined the army, became an officer in Intelligence, and in 1943 died mysteriously by gunshot in a train *en route* from Jerusalem to Cairo. Beside him there was a copy of the medieval French *Tristan and Iseult*. He was thirty-two.

His best-known book. *I'll Go to Bed at Noon*, published posthumously in 1944, was a short sequence of letters to his sons; it was given its title partly because, like a great many other people at that time, he thought he might die young, partly because 'I'll go to bed at noon' were the last words he spoke on the stage. The letters were written to his children, who had been evacuated to the United States, and they speak of matters forced on his attention by the shocks of the summer of 1940; the French surrender on 24 June compelled everybody to do some thinking about the unthinkable. Haggard's thoughts are not very remarkable—he dwells on the necessity of resistance, on the disappointment of visionary hopes, on the wasted sacrifices of 1914–18. He is baffled by the pacifists, and asks what the next generation will think of that 'race of unwilling traitors'. For the most part the book is passionate, sincere, and commonplace, as most works of this kind would have been at the time. But there are some less ordinary fragments of autobiography. He tells his sons that as an adolescent he had feared women, and that as a child he had never had 'a proper home'; his father worked abroad as consul-general in New York. He also gives a sensitive description of his first love-affair, which happened in Germany.

Haggard's friend Christopher Hassall wrote an introduction to *I'll Go to Bed at Noon*, and later published a biography, from which I have taken these details.[12] Hassall tells us that *Nya* was a sex-changed self-portrait; the girl's school experiences were adapted from those undergone by the author at Haileybury; a sympathetic schoolmistress is based on Wilfrid Blunt, his friend among the masters. Haggard himself was also the model for Simon. We are told that he passed through public school in total sexual ignorance; it was only when, at the age of nineteen, he visited Munich in the company of Blunt that he first discovered 'the most rudimentary of the "facts of life" '; so Blunt testifies. On a visit to Venice Haggard came to know

---

[11] As reported in the *Observer*, 24 Aug. 1986.   [12] *The Timeless Quest* (1948).

Lowes Dickinson and Roger Fry. Back home, he went to RADA, to launch his first career. By 1938 he was not only a successful actor but a man of much amorous experience, said indeed to be 'irresistible to women'. Yet in choosing to be a writer he began with an idyll of sexual inexperience.

Haggard thought seriously about altering the end of *Nya* or writing a sequel—he would bring Simon back from the United States some years later, with a wife, to be met by Nya on the arm of a fiancé. The publisher discouraged this addition. During his army service Haggard wrote another novel or novella called *The Magnolia Tree*, which was never published.[13] Hassall says it is a self-portrait at the age of forty-five; the subject looks back on a love-affair with a Swiss girl visiting England, an affair interrupted by the German invasion of the Low Countries in May 1940. The epiphanies of love were now thoroughly mixed up with the events of contemporary history. Another autobiographical novel, *The Wave and the Moon*, was left unfinished; according to Hassall it was to be 'twice as long as *Gone with the Wind*'. Its third part was to be called 'If Love be Pain', and it was to represent a 'return to instinct' after the confusions of a second part in which 'intellect takes control' and 'everything goes wrong'. Haggard also wrote poems, some of them posthumously published. One of them crops up in Brian Gardner's anthology of Second World War poetry, *The Terrible Rain* (1966). Dated 'Cairo, 1943', it must have been written shortly before his death. It is a love-poem, and by no means a bad one. It does not mention the war.

Haggard's short life illustrates a theme which, as I've said, became unusually important in the Thirties. The issue is of class consciousness, or rather consciousness of one's relation to another class; or unconsciousness that such a relation was called for, and the sudden intrusion of that need into consciousness. Haggard's family background was such that he inevitably went to public school and shared the benefits and privations of his class. They show in his work as well as in his life. From half the world—women—he had lived as a youth in a condition of uneasy estrangement, like his Simon. He was equally cut off from, and quite ignorant of, the plight of the poor. The war changed him, but it also killed him before he could become a different sort of writer, less subject to accusations of sentimentality

---

[13] According to Sir Geoffrey, it was too short for economy production according to the rules obtaining at the time; it was also lacking in movement.

and complacency, or whatever the silent charges against him may be: less constricted, shall we say, by the assumptions he meant to challenge. Certainly his novel lacks wickedness, is unable to be shocking; his dangerous subject is rendered quite safe. He mimes transgression but never crosses the boundary.

Nya was not the first under-age beloved in modern literature. If novels truly reflected life there might be many of them, but there are always reasons why novels don't do that. Of J. L. Carter's novel *The Nymphet*, published in 1915, I have been unable to find a copy, but Malcolm Bradbury, who has lost his, wrote an account of it before he did so.[14] It is about an eleven-year-old girl, the nymphet of the title, and her relations with a successful playwright; but he takes an interest in the girl only because he is pursuing her elder sister. However, the little girl is also a child of nature, and likes to think of sailing away with her man.

Carter wasn't using the word 'nymphet' in its modern sense, which is entirely due to Nabokov. In the *Oxford English Dictionary* the old sense is illustrated from Drayton—young nymph or little nymph—whereas the *Supplement* very properly gives Nabokov's own definition: 'Between the age limits of nine and fourteen there occur maidens who, to certain bewitched travellers, twice or many times as old as they, reveal their true nature, which is not human, but nymphic (that is, demoniac) and these chosen creatures I propose to designate as "nymphets".'

Only seventeen years (in addition, of course, to the differences of education enjoyed by the authors) separate *Nya* from *Lolita*. There were initially some doubts about the propriety of Nabokov's book, which is why it was first published in Paris and by the Olympia Press, but nowadays it is commonly praised for its reticence. All the same, it does not compete in reticence with Haggard's novel. It may seem over-obvious to compare these books, but I think there may be rewards for doing so. Both treat of a sexual relationship which, if consummated, is against the law of the countries in which the stories are set, and would probably be offensive to most citizens of those countries even if it were not. It is true that there have been exceptions: Ernest Dowson, for instance, was put out when, in 1885, the

---

[14] In *Mademoiselle*, May, 1963. I am grateful to Mr Bradbury for sending me a copy of this article.

age of consent was raised from thirteen to sixteen (only ten years earlier it had been raised from twelve to thirteen); he complained about 'the English tradition which assumes Heaven knows why? that a girl is not Amabilis when she is at her most amiable age.'[15] For him, too, it was irritating to live in a country organized entirely in favour of grown-up people. And we can easily think of other lovers of little girls, some innocent and some not. But mostly we are against this kind of thing, and, as Lionel Trilling put it in his memorable review of *Lolita* (1955), 'the breaking of the taboo about the sexual unavailability of young girls has for us something of the force that a wife's infidelity had for Shakespeare'.[16]

Trilling notes a diminution in the public capacity for indignation between the time of Joyce and Lawrence and that of *Lolita*, but he insists that in its own way Nabokov's is a shocking book—not pornographic, but shocking because it violates that taboo. And he says that to write a love-story nowadays you need to abandon all thought of normal modern sexual relations. You need a love that somehow defies normality, that has nothing to do with stability, mutuality, or the other standards by which the success of a modern marriage is measured. The love Nabokov treats of in *Lolita* is just such a love, as aberrant as that of Tristan and Isolde; that it is pathological is the condition of its being genuine. Humbert really does adore his cold young mistress—you can feel it as he watches her playing tennis, and hear it when he later threatens her husband with reprisals for any ill-treatment she may suffer. He even has some paternal feelings, he even has some sense of guilt, in spite of his knowledge that he was not the girl's first lover.

But as readers we don't moralize this book; instead we notice that

[15] *The Letters of Ernest Dowson*, ed. D. Flower and H. Maas (1967), 187, 221.

[16] Reprinted in L. Trilling, *Speaking of Literature and Society*, ed. D. Trilling (1980), 221. It should probably be remarked that there is a long literary tradition of poems about very young girls. A familiar example is Marvell's 'To Little T.C. in a Prospect of Flowers', and J. B. Leishman traces the theme back to the Greek Anthology (*The Art of Marvell's Poetry* (1966), 163–89). *Lolita* is a very literary book, and Nabokov had earlier used similar themes as part of what his editor, Alfred Appel jun., calls his 'strategy of involution' (*The Annotated Lolita* (1970), p. xxvi). Appel also remarks that a book by Nabokov is at least to some extent 'allégorique de lui-même', as Mallarmé said of his work (p. xxii). We hardly need reminding that, in so far as the novel is about its own involutions, it isn't about child abuse, but in the present context the intensely wrought artifice of Nabokov's novel is worth remembering for the contrast it offers to *Nya*, which can hardly be described, in the words Nabokov used of *Lolita*, as 'a beautiful puzzle' (quoted in Appel, p. xi).

for Nabokov at least it was true that the lunatic, the lover, and the poet were of imagination all compact. The lover is a sort of criminal lunatic, his book is the work of a poet; his crazy self-regard, his gluttonous sexual appetite, his comic degradation, are reflected in the self-regarding surface of the book, with all its jokes and covert allusions, its reachings after an 'aesthetic bliss' to match the bliss of Humbert as he makes love to a feverish child in a motel room. The novel succeeds by transgressions of fictional norms and contracts as wanton and lawless as the transgressions of its characters.

Lolita, then, is, by comparison with *Nya*, transgressive through and through. Both are love-stories, but Haggard's is not of the kind Trilling thought proper to modern times, and Nabokov's is. If we consider the centrality, in earlier novels, of adultery, we may conclude that changes in moral climate force the transgressor to raise his stakes, to find a taboo still worth violating. William Empson, writing about *Othello*, remarked that 'the advent of contraceptives has taken a lot of strain off the topic' of adultery.[17] Shakespeare would nowadays need to find new ways to shock.

Tony Tanner, in his book *Adultery in the Novel* (1979), argues extensively the point that fiction is intimately related to sexual transgression, which is reflexively enacted in fictional forms. That the bourgeois novel is obsessed with adultery is simply a consequence of its socio-historical placement. The myths of transgression lie much deeper, as deep, perhaps, as Empson's 'permanent truths'. There is, for example, an ancient obligation on guests not to disturb the social and ethical order into which they are received; the taboo may be reflected in the double sense of the Latin word *hostis*, connoting both a guest and an outsider, an enemy; in switching from the latter to the former sense the guest silently accepts a taboo on the host's women. Because Paris broke this variously manifested rule we have the *Iliad*. Tanner believes that its violation is 'one of the permanently generative themes of Western literature', citing Tristan, Lancelot, Polixenes, Iachimo, and Heathcliff as instances of guest–ousiders who transgress, or wish to transgress, or are suspected of transgressing (p. 26).[18] Here is a taboo with some of the

---

[17] *The Structure of Complex Words* (1951), 245.
[18] Dr A. D. Nuttall tells me that he was troubled by this passage in my lecture, finding the argument about *hostis* implausible; he thinks the real ambiguity in Latin is rather in the senses of *hospes*. Benveniste, Tanner's authority and consequently mine, argues (in part) as follows: 'The term *hostis* will here be considered in its relations with

force of the incest prohibition; and perhaps the seduction of under-
age girls is merely an aspect of it, more shocking to us in our time
than the forms in which it appeared in older literature.

Tanner's point is that the force which disrupts the household or
the social order is also the force that launches and drives on the
narrative. It is an uncontrolled, and from the normal point of view a
perverted, erotic impulse, what Lovelace, another intruder, is talking about when he says that 'love, that deserves the name, never was
under the dominion of prudence, or of any reasoning power'. Its
force drives it across settled boundaries: boundaries that separate
brother from sister, the welcomed guest from the wife, the grown
man from the pubescent girl, or—by a transference I shall discuss
later—the rich from the poor. The entire civilization is threatened;
and the violation of the familiar by some other, the stranger, is the
force that makes the necessary moment of disequilibrium in which
narrative begins; the fiction which permanently interests us is a
struggle at or across a frontier, it chronicles, happily or otherwise,
the ravages of the stranger in conflict with the settled order.

All this may do something to explain why *Nya* failed the test of
time, whereas *Lolita* appears to be doing well. Haggard's book
makes some mild protests against the social order, but is always keen
to preserve its decency; Nabokov's hero is a ribald stranger, fascinated not only by the otherness of Lolita and her weird youth
culture, but also by the otherness of the United States, the seductive
freedoms of its highways, motels, language, and diet. He is every-
where and in everything guest and stranger (enemy, violator). Like
Heathcliff and Lovelace, he is invading somebody else's space, not
merely parleying with the immigration officers. The difference
is not that Haggard's characters have more conscience than

other Latin words of the same family. . . . but we will leave aside *hospes*, which,
although it seems to be related, has not been analysed with any certainty.' The word
hostis still meant 'stranger' in the Law of the XII Tables, and this sense was familiar to
learned Romans. Varro and Festus explain that among the ancients people were called
'hostes' who were, though foreigners, granted equal civic rights with Romans, and
were thus both strangers and guests. It was when the ties of citizenship were
strengthened, and it came to seem anomalous that non-Romans might enjoy similar
rights to those who were properly of the *civitas*, that the sense altered and the stranger
became an enemy (Émile Benveniste, *Problèmes de linguistique générale* (1966), 320–1).
So there seems to be some evidence for the primitive fusion of the senses 'guest' and
'stranger enjoying reciprocal rights of hospitality', though the exact nature of both the
fusion and the dissociation must be to a considerable degree conjectural.

Nabokov's. Humbert Humbert is pitiless in self-gratification, but he also speaks of 'this horror that I cannot shake off'; in *Nya* nobody experiences guilt, the text of the book does not disturb us by foreign antics, and we are no more upset than the placid uncle or the understanding schoolmistress. For interesting otherness, demonic transgressiveness, one has to look elsewhere. *Nya* is not concerned with difference of sex or class—it is, virtually, a one-sex, one-class book; it subscribes to the current civilized morality, is almost complicit with Aunt Ethel. Simon dreads the thought of arousing Nya; the servants—a housemaid who befriends Nya, and the long-shoreman who sails off with Simon—are pastoral props. Nya herself is tamed by her middle-class school and her middle-class household, and knows it is right to be so tamed, right that the pipe-smokers and bridge-players should intercept the potion and exile Tristan. It is what Forster called going into the dark. When Nya broke Simon's pipe it seemed that their lives might change. But he soon got a new pipe, the demon didn't break in; and Nya seems headed for a life of tennis and bridge, with a husband who hides behind *The Times*.

And, as I said, I suppose one reason for my having liked it—and remembering it because I liked it, because of the unusual situation in which I read it—was just because it treated so calmly its potentially explosive subject; it assumed so quietly that the English bourgeoisie could confidently contain such terrible forces. Yet it was written at a time when the middle class was being assailed by doubts and terrors and alien intrusions of an intensity it had never before experienced. The sheer docility of the book is bound to seem an image of larger evasions, for example of the differences in one's own back yard, between the unemployed to the north and the well-to-do in the south-east; or between comfortable England and riven Europe. The conflicts, the demonic boundary-crossers, were far away, in Spain and Austria and 'where Poland draws her eastern bow'. The book contains no word of imminent hostile inroads, no monsters; and the love-story, in the way of its telling, neutralizes all fear, all awe, of the other sex. The poor and the enemy were like sexual others; un-known, perhaps unknowable, terribly mature, but always in the wings of the book, obscene, kept off-stage by decency; by bridge, ocean voyages, regressions into latency.

Other writers, whom for one reason or another we remember better, came to think such docility conscienceless, and wished to deal honestly with the dangers and the allurements, with the problems of 'the ladies and gentlemen apart, too much alone'; and of the poor, also apart, possessors of a strange, possibly a splendid alien culture. They saw a need to cross frontiers, however costly and dangerous the transit. Some of them died in the attempt, and some of them retreated; not, in my view, ignominiously. It is to some of those writers, and to their dealings with these strangers, that I shall turn in the next chapter.

2 · On the Frontier

I HAVE suggested that, at any rate in some measure, literature which achieves permanence is likely to be 'transgressive' and that in periods like the Thirties fiction in particular tends to be more vigorous when it works on or across certain frontiers, notably those of sex and class. The literature of the Thirties is well known to have a special interest in borders and frontiers, and there flourished in some important writers a conscientious conviction that borders and frontiers must be crossed. I suggested that one's sense that Haggard's novel is of limited value arises at least in part from its acquiescence in a class ideology it only pretends to challenge, from its acceptance of frontiers as interesting but inviolable; so that its potentially transgressive theme—a love which violates a deep prohibition—is tamed, it capitulates to middle-class decency. *Lolita*, on the other hand, is sinister, carnavalesque, a lone raider; it contemptuously or wantonly violates frontiers—and we can include among them the temporal horizon within which it was conceived; for it is still, after more than thirty years, capable of surprising or even shocking the reader.

I want now to develop the theme of sexual and social divisions in the Thirties. The public school seems an obvious place to begin. Perhaps I should say that I'm not talking about public schools as they are now, or even necessarily as they were then, but only of the way in which writers of left-wing tendencies saw them. There are many memoirs recounting the miseries of schooldays, and some of them are by writers of great distinction—though I have heard it argued that it was only the boys who were going to become writers who suffered so badly. However this may be, I begin by saying something concerning a now-forgotten public-school novel for which, as I remember, my contemporaries had in those days considerable respect. Arthur Calder-Marshall's *Dead Centre*, published in 1935, describes, with a certain originality of form, the vicissitudes of a school year. One of its themes is a difference of opinion about the methods and purposes of this kind of education. A younger generation of teachers seeks responsibility for the general spiritual and cultural welfare of the boys. The older generation believes it is enough to instruct them, to lay down inflexible rules and see that they are observed. The rest may be left to the boys themselves; the master's responsibilities end at the school gates. To go beyond that is 'impertinent interference'. Such masters have no interest in life outside the school; it is their world, and their loyalties are owed to the school rather than to its transient inmates and the world into which they will pass. But the young masters do not intend to stay so long, and are conscious of a desire to 'flee to the educated world'.

Dead Centre tries among other things to give one an idea of what it means to live in a world of education that is cut off from the educated world, or simply from the world at large. The great events of the year are the death of an idolized boy in an accident on a rugby-tackling machine, and another boy's running away from school because he has, or may have, impregnated one of the maids. Such girls can be intensely attractive, but, as one of the boys remarks of the maid of his choice, 'she's really vulgar and her voice is common and she's full of silly affectations that fill me with shame when I remember them'. The book gives one a quite strong sense of the poverty of its isolated society, a poverty both economic (the masters are ill-paid) and emotional. Of the marriages of members of staff only one is represented as satisfactory, that of the proletarian cricket professional.

Calder-Marshall's school is called 'Richbury', with the straightforward suggestion that it is, in relation to the world about it, a rich enclave, but also with a certain irony that it should be, inside the frontiers of privilege, so poor a place. Others responded quite differently to the condition of privileged isolation—Cyril Connolly saw Eton in retrospect as 'a far more weird and privileged and threatened and vanishing society than ever I realised'. *Enemies of Promise* was published in 1938, in the week of the Munich Agreement, and Connolly was entitled to a certain nostalgia for a world that seemed without question to be disappearing for ever; but Orwell, who was at Eton at the same time, thought this sentiment ridiculous. He also gave an account of the prep. school they both attended, an account antithetical to Connolly's and probably a bit darker than the facts would justify. But the disagreement concerned the effects of weirdness and privilege, not their existence. Connolly remembered his last year at Eton as a premature life climax; Orwell thought public schools a national and social disaster. Neither would

24

dispute that such schools catered for the privileged and were
dedicated to the continuation of privilege.

Bernard Bergonzi has argued that they grew more powerful in the
years between the wars, with the result that the writers of the
Thirties give evidence of an increase in 'cultural homogeneity' over
those of the previous generation.[1] At any rate it is clear enough that
the difference between the prospects of the beneficiaries of privilege,
however wretched some claim to have been, and those of the
remainder of the population, had come to seem greater. With luck
the privilege might last for life, and so might one's isolation from the
world. School, followed by Oxford or Cambridge, would probably
at least ensure that one didn't join the unemployed, from whom
one was in any case sharply distinguished by accent, dress, and,
sometimes, sexual preference.

In such circumstances fear and suspicion of the outsider could be
intensified, and, if you were inside the fortifications of privilege,
where school fees for one term could be more than a working-class
family had to live on for a year, you might think it prudent to
strengthen those fortifications. Calder-Marshall was one of the
writers who found this cold class war disturbing, as he demonstrated
in a more ambitious novel, also much admired in its time, called *Pie
in the Sky* (1937); it contains many instances of social injustice, for
example by magistrates dealing with unemployed men tramping the
roads in search of work. Then there was the Means Test. I suppose it
is impossible for anybody under sixty to imagine how the unemployed felt about the Means Test, which penalized them for having
saved a little money against the hard times that were now upon
them. It was an indignity that seemed intolerable to bourgeois
sympathizers, and in the writing of the time it was always execrated;
though I see that A. J. P. Taylor, in his volume of the *Oxford History
of England*, contemplates it without passion, treating it as a
bureaucratic muddle that came out quite well in the end.[2] He does,
however, remark that it caused 'the trenches of class war' to 'run
along the floor of the house of commons'. It marked another
boundary between hostile powers.

The middle class could ease its mind by refusing to believe in
poverty, or by regarding it as self-inflicted. Since most of the worst
suffering took place well away from London, and had to be drama-

[1] *Reading the Thirties* (1978), 10.   [2] (1965), 352–4.

tized by hunger marches, this defence was fairly easy to maintain. There were, however, those whose consciences did not allow them this option, and among them were those 'bourgeois intellectuals' thought by some to be traitors to their class. Being interested in modern art and modern thought, they felt isolated even in their own class; and their rapidly developing interest in the working class rarely extended to any close acquaintance. They had inherited among their privileges habits of obscurity and frivolity that were hard to give up, even though conscience seemed to require it, and intelligence perceived that the dikes of content were threatening to burst. They invented their own social order, and formed associations which survived school and university. They wrote of and to one another in semi-private languages, played their own quasi-surrealistic games. Such were the friendships of Isherwood, Upward, and Auden. It was with talents developed in these ways that they approached the task imposed upon them by the times—to cross no-man's-land, to fraternize in the proletarian trenches.

Conscience insisted they seek some kind of genuine meeting with the workers, with the unknown, the wholly other; and the need for such a relationship presented itself as one of necessary love. Lord Annan tells us that the period between the wars was the highwater mark of gentlemanly homosexuality,[3] and that accounts for at least some of the ways in which solidarity with the workers found expression. Christopher Isherwood tells us that he and his friends found themselves at odds with 'Nearly Everybody'; England was 'the land of the Others', and he felt obliged to seek a homeland elsewhere, at first in Germany. Christopher, he says, 'couldn't relax sexually with his own class or nation. He needed a working-class foreigner.' He needed also recognition of his proudly ambiguous sexual status, and he found it at the Hirschfeld Institute in Berlin, where homosexuals were regarded as a Third Sex. For all this he was willing to resign from what he called 'the family'—his class and his country. Being himself upperclass, Christopher despised the middle class for 'aping' upper-class manners. 'That left him with nothing to admire but the working class, so he declared it to be forthright, without frills, altogether on the path of truth,' especially if it was foreign.[4]

[3] *New York Review of Books*, 20 Nov. 1986.
[4] *Christopher and his Kind* (1977), 10, 27.

Isherwood is here writing almost half a century after the event, his leftish days very far in the past, and he may be caricaturing his younger self, but there is some plausibility in the portrait. He is explaining his reasons for self-exile and for loving workers. Behind all the promiscuities he was willing, years later, to recount, there was a persistent need for 'the ideal companion to whom you can reveal yourself totally and yet be loved for what you are, not what you pretend to be'. Such a friend is unlikely, for the reasons Isherwood has given, to be of one's own guarded class. It is obvious from Isherwood's writings and from those of his friends that such lovers were cherished, their claims taking precedence over everything else. Not everybody thought this a useful state of affairs. Claud Cockburn once remarked that

the intellectual homosexual of those days was really like an early nineteenth-century romantic—however political he might think himself, everything had to give place to his *amour*; for some reason this was considered respectable when it was a boy although it would have been laughable had it been a girl. Just as one thought he was going to sit down and write an article for a magazine, or go to Spain, it turned out he was getting his boy friend out of the hands of the police. This was a number one priority. Homosexuality had a sort of prestige value that took precedence over politics, the end of the world, and everything else.[5]

The quest for the Ideal Friend (this time mostly at home) is extensively described in J. R. Ackerley's book *My Father and Myself*, published in the candid year of 1968. 'Though two or three hundred young men were to pass through my hands in the course of years I did not consider myself promiscuous but monogamous, it was all a run of bad luck,' he says (p. 109). His specifications for the Ideal Friend were so exigent that it eventually became clear that nobody could meet them. 'It may be thought', he adds, 'that the reason why this search was taking me out of my own class . . . was that guilt in sex obliged me to work it off on my social inferiors' (p. 110). If so, the obligation was easily met, for sailors and guardsmen were always short of cash.

Reviewing Ackerley's books, Auden explained what was likely to happen in the course of the quest for the Ideal Friend. The seeker is looking for a beloved who is 'in some way "other" than the lover'. Heterosexuals are fortunate in that their desire for otherness is

[5] 'A Conversation with Claud Cockburn', *Review*, 11–12 (1965), 52.

satisfied by natural sexual differences. The homosexual man may, if he is lucky, content himself with such lesser differences as occur in different physical types, such as Sheldon's mesomorph and ecto-morph. But trouble begins when the difference desired is psycho-logical or cultural. The intellectual and relatively well-off homosexual like Ackerley is apt to 'become romantically enchanted with the working class, whose lives, experiences and interests are so different from his own, and to whom, because they are poorer, the money and comforts he is able to provide can be a cause for affectionate gratitude'. And that may, for a time, be enough. But a permanent relationship demands not only a union of othernesses but some interests held in common. Soon the intellectual gets bored, and his quest begins again, leading him into what looks to non-questers like extraordinary promiscuity.[6] This is interesting but not the whole story. According to Francis King, his executor, Ackerley, 'like many other homosexuals of his generation . . . combined a sexual passion for the male working-classes with a thorough-going contempt for them. . . . They were lazy, dishonest, incompetent, selfish, money-grubbing.'[7] As we saw, Ackerley himself suspected that there was an ambiguity of this sort in his attitude to his lovers, and a blend of passion and contempt is possibly a more likely formula than Auden's enchantment leading to boredom. In the event Ackerley gave up the quest, fell in love with a dog, and had fifteen years of cloudless happiness. His solution satisfies the requirement of otherness, though hardly that of common cultural interests. As a substitute for a working-class lover, Tulip would not have done for everybody.

Ackerley provides us with a symbolic representation of the blend-ing or perhaps the confusion of sex and class. The desire for permanence, as a need overriding other needs, may have been a bit newfangled: Ackerley's combination of old-style contemptuous exploitation with a desire for permanence suggest a state of tran-sition. Gide's Immoralist long before said that 'the society of the lowest dregs of humanity was delectable company to me; and what need had I to understand their language when I felt it in my whole body?'[8] But Gide, remembering his Moroccan adventures, was not

---

[6] *Forewords and Afterwords*, ed. E. Mendelson (1973), 450 ff.
[7] J. R. Ackerley, *My Sister and Myself*, ed. F. King (1982), 20.
[8] *L'Immoraliste* (1902), trans. D. Bussy (1930), 196.

under the influence of E. M. Forster. The kind of delectable encounter Gide enjoyed was still easily available, and still much sought after;
but there was also this serious though transgressive quest, prompted
in part by conscience. The quest for the Ideal Friend can be the image
of a politics, and so, of course, can its abandonment.

These problems were by no means peculiar to homosexuals;
people whose contempt for bourgeois notions of love combined
with a passionate wish to identify themselves with the workers
might also run into them. In his trilogy *The Spiral Ascent* (1977), to
which I shall return at more length in the next chapter, Edward
Upward describes the love-affair and subsequent marriage of a poor
but upper-class young writer with a working-class schoolteacher.
They get to know each other at the local Party branch—it is difficult
to imagine them meeting anywhere else—and they later set up house
together in a dismal maisonette. Looking around this mean apartment, and then turning to his girlfriend, the young man cries out,
quite involuntarily, 'Oh Elsie, you're so ugly!' But he overcomes his
repugnance as a gesture of solidarity with her class. What happened
was that the bourgeois idea of love was replaced by an equally
fantastic idea, that the workers were, despite any appearance to the
contrary, intrinsically and tragically beautiful. Upward's couple do
have interests in common—the Party, parenthood, much later
CND. The young man badly misses his writing, which seems to call
for some bourgeois peace and solitude, but thinks he could not write
well in any case if he lost touch with the Party and the class his wife
comes to represent. He associates the ugliness of the maisonette with
her ugliness, but it is finally the beauty of her class that makes her
beautiful and lovable.

There is surely something distinctive here, something for which
one can't easily think of parallels in other periods. The relations of
the well-to-do with their inferiors had been simpler, more conde-
scending (in the good lost sense as well as the bad current one),
probably more exploitative; certainly less loving. Munby and his
housemaid–wife come to mind as a possible exception; but she
belonged to the kitchen and he to the drawing room, and the
marriage was secret. Engels had his working-class mistress, Zola his
laundress, indeed such arrangements were commonplace; but, affectionate as they doubtless very often were, unions of that sort were
founded on inequalities of class and income. It would be ridiculous to
suggest that such relationships were suddenly eliminated or trans-

formed by the bourgeois Communists of the Thirties; there has probably never been a time when one couldn't buy whatever one could conceivably desire, as in Auden's Red Light district, where they advertise 'girls of eighty and women of four' as well as 'boys of every shape and size'.[9] And less commercially, there were arrangements of the kind described by Gerald Brenan in his genial memoirs, adventures with the class of women known generically as 'shopgirls' —sub-bohemian, unemployed, or underpaid, available for decent, uncommitted relationships quite free of the constraints of middle-class morality.[10] The old style persisted; but it does look as though something new was overtaking it. There was a new perception of innocence and virtue in the workers; Upward is like Montaigne writing about the cannibals, not in the least like Hazlitt in his frenzy or Brenan with his amiable pick-ups.

An impressive early version of the new style—American but applicable—is Edmund Wilson's story 'The Princess with the Golden Hair' (in *Memoirs of Hecate County* (1946)). The narrator, an art gallery official, is involved in two affairs, one with a working girl and one with an upper-class woman. The rich lady represents a bogus bourgeois culture; she is a perversely unsatisfactory lover, and wears a brace to alleviate an imaginary back ailment. The working girl is real—though he picks her up in the Brenan manner, her natural common sense forces him to revise his theoretical notions of the proletariat, and he gains through her some understanding of the lives and landscapes of the poor. The other woman gives an ordinary view of such affairs—'So you got yourself a girl on Fourteenth Street and became a crusader for the working class! So that's what your Marxism is made of!' And he does deplore her slovenly speech, and he does acknowledge an element of sadistic exploitation in his attitude; and he does lose her. But he admits that it was she who gave him

> that life of the people which had before been but prices and wages, legislation and technical progress. . . . She had given me this vision—I had lived on it . . . and she had given me something else. . . . It was somehow

---

[9] *The Dog beneath the Skin* (1937), 57, 58. Edward Mendelson writes to inform me that 'the whole nightclub scene in *The Dog beneath the Skin*, with the chorus of "Fair girls, dear girls, Dark girls, stark girls", etc., offering themselves for the audience's delight, was simply a resexed and otherwise adjusted version of part of the revue Auden wrote for the boys of the Downs School a few weeks before'.

[10] *A Life of One's Own* (1962, 1975); *Personal Record* (1974).

the true sanction for life. . . . It was something so strong and instinctive that
it could outlive the hurts and infections, the defilements, among which we
lived—so organic that it could not be analyzed. She had transmitted a belief
and a beauty that could not be justified or explained.[11]

To love the worker was not only to love a newly discovered class but
to burst through into a new and more genuine world.

There is an old kind of poetry called the 'pastourelle', usually giving
a boastful account of a knight's or a poet's success with a peasant girl
encountered in the countryside. Although the girl sometimes resists
and sometimes turns the tables on the gentleman, the affair is a sort of
gentle rape, dignified in the Provençal versions with some amorous
metaphysics. One could use the term 'pastourelle' for the old style of
sexual plundering. A different way of treating the lives and loves of
the peasant is 'pastoral', in which there is a general assumption that
lower-class characters are not only simpler but purer than their
betters, and for that reason constitute a proper subject of upper-class
study; as Empson put it, 'you can say everything about complex
people by a complete consideration of simple people'.[12] Of course in
doing so you use means far from simple. But I think we could say
that the change in attitude towards working-class lovers, the transformation I've postulated, is in a way a switch from pastourelle to
pastoral.

   Here is another illustration of the difference, this time from
Austria. Robert Musil has a story 'Grigia', about the seduction of a
peasant woman by a landowner; it gives a virtuoso description of
their love-making in a hayloft, and ends with the husband's revenge.
This is a form of pastourelle. Musil's 'Tonka', a longer and subtler
tale, is what we can all recognize as a version of pastoral. A student
has an affair with a shopgirl. He 'loved her because he did not love
her, because she did not stir his soul, but rinsed it clean and
smooth. . . . She was Nature adjusting itself to Mind, not wanting
to become Mind, but loving it and inscrutably attaching itself to it.'
Others, of course, think of Tonka as 'a common little thing who
used to work in a shop'. She turns out to be, in her simplicity, as
complex as the civilized could possibly imagine, both honourable
and treacherous. Since her pregnancy is accompanied by a venereal

[11] 'The Princess with the Golden Hair', in *Memoirs of Hecate County* (1942; rev. edn.
1959), 242, 31.   [12] *Some Versions of Pastoral* (1935), 4–5.

infection she has certainly been unfaithful; yet after her death the
young man feels her 'from the ground under his feet to the crown of
his head, and the whole of her life. . . . From that time on much
came to his mind that made him a little better than other
people . . .'[13]

Here we are quite close to the Wilson version; he gives a rather
similar situation an allegorical dressing. In both stories the bourgeois
lover finds his whole life enriched by a proletarian mistress. Musil, as
we know from his great unfinished novel, was fascinated by the idea
that the erotic transformation of consciousness is the archetype of all
other transformations of consciousness. The many sexual combi-
nations exhibited in *The Man without Qualities* (1930–2) testify to the
great truth that all knowledge of the other, all intercourse between
opposites, is analogous to carnal knowledge. It is an idea ready for
political applications. The love between individuals who represent
collectivities, classes, is a union of political opposites that aspires to
inseparability, androgyny. One of Musil's women has a passion for
an androgyne Greek, and this passion also has political analogues.

The hermaphrodite as emblem of inseparable union has ancient
roots, notably of course in Plato, but it has long had political as well
as carnal connotations: on the one hand Gautier with his boy–girl
Mlle de Maupin, Balzac's *Séraphîtâ*, and *Sarrasine*, and on the other
the Saint-Simonians; the sexual (including, according to Barthes,[14]
the Sadist–sexual) lends its erotic charge to the political. Homosexuals could think of themselves as belonging to Hirschfeld's 'Third
Sex', as in themselves androgynous; heterosexual lovers are capable
of imagining their union in the same way. These Utopias are of all
kinds, to be found in Auden's accommodating brothel ('Here Plato's
halves are at last united'[15]) and in visions of the undivided society.
Union with the Ideal Friend, union with the proletariat: these also
could have the hermaphrodite as emblem.[16]

---

[13] R. Musil, *Four Women*, trans. E. Wilkins and E. Kaiser (1966), 89, 86, 122.

[14] He says that the characteristically modern perversity founded by De Sade
requires an effort to do away with the sex of the woman, and change her, as nearly as
possible, into a boy; but she cannot be what she is Other than, and so becomes an
ambiguous figure whom it is a transgression to touch. The libertine's desire is to
pervert 'object, word and organ' from its ordinary usage (*Sade, Fourier, Loyola* (1971),
127).

[15] *The Dog beneath the Skin*, p. 57.

[16] See A. J. L. Busst, 'The Image of the Androgyne in the Nineteenth Century', in
Ian Fletcher (ed.), *Romantic Mythologies* (1967), 1–95.

Accounts of such hoped-for unions are written by only one of the
two persons, and the writer, like Sade's libertine, cannot in fact make
of his subject what he or she is other than. And in such cases the
writer is always the complex person looking at an Other, whose
complexity is made evident only by that look. Such is pastoral when
it is about the possibility of love between classes. Empson published
his book on pastoral in 1935; having seen the relevance of the genre to
contemporary feelings about class, he placed at the beginning of the
book his chapter on the proletarian novel. He doesn't seem to have
read many such novels, remarking only in a general way that those
he had come across were not much good; but he still made what must
be the essential points. Empson was always interested in what look
like irreconcilable opposites, the division between science and
poetry, between lovers, between the halves of metaphor and the
constituents of double plots, and it must have seemed obvious in
1935 that the divided classes could be added to this list. However, he
was fairly sure that attempts to bring the classes together in some
future happiness would prove difficult, would produce results not
desired by the propagandists, and introduce some ambiguities into
their propaganda. Hence the unintentional Fascism he detected in
Auden's *Spain*: today political necessity compels us to condone 'the
necessary murder' but tomorrow, when the struggle is won, we can
hope to have 'fun under | Liberty's masterful shadow', rediscover
romantic love, and so forth. Empson, drawing on his knowledge of
the Chinese, temperately observes that he 'can't feel that the race of
man is like this at all. What is heartening about people is their
appalling stubbornness and the strong roots of their various cultures,
rather than the ease with which you can convert them and make
them happy and good. Probably a whole political outlook can turn
on this.' And he shrewdly adds, 'Maybe you could connect the
utopian note of the politics [in *Spain*] with a remark in one of the
love-poems [of Auden]:

> I believed for years that
> Love was the conjunction
> Of two oppositions;
>   That was all untrue . . .'[17]

[17] Empson's review of Auden's *Another Time*, in J. Haffenden (ed.), *W. H. Auden: The Critical Heritage* (1983), 306.

The conjunction of opposites represented by the very words 'proletarian' and 'novel' struck him as presenting special difficulties. In his discussion of Gray's 'Elegy' he notes that the bourgeois 'surface' of the poem contains the false suggestion that 'for the poor man things cannot be improved in any degree', but that under the surface there is a 'permanent truth': the inevitable loss and waste in any human life. Bourgeois poetry can thus be true and false at the same time; and indeed the big question is, whether a great poetic statement can *possibly* be true without being bourgeois–false.

One sees how the times were bearing down on this very independent mind. Empson comes close to saying that the truth about the working class can *only* be told by bourgeois writers—'good proletarian art is usually Covert Pastoral'. Novels by working-class writers are not pastoral, but they are either bad or by writers 'trying to break out of the proletariat into the intelligentsia, or rather the lower middle classes into the upper'. (This was also the view of Orwell.) Pastoral, then, however unsatisfactory, is the only way the working class can be written about, as it must be if we are to have that union so much desired. Empson notices the sexual analogy, and quotes, with scepticism, Radek's speech, which in 1934 inaugurated socialist realism by saying that proletarian literature will be a literature of love for the oppressed. But that literature would not be written by proletarians. The heroic worker, for instance, is not a working-class perception, and if a working-class writer put such a figure in a book he would be ceasing to act like a member of his class. In the end Empson puts the whole thing quite simply, and perhaps too generally: since no artist is ever at one with his public, no artist can be a worker. He allows the possibility that to be any good the artist 'should be in contact with the worker', but even so the result will be pastoral. It seems that this is the only way workers can get into books.[18]

On this view the problem of how to tell the truth about workers, or even provide a suitable set of useful lies, is about as old as Theocritus. But, when the proletariat (a term not used of modern industrial workers until the second half of the nineteenth century) became the subject of pastoral (rather than shepherds, fishermen, etc.), everything changed, for modern political economy was directly involved; and in the political climate of the Thirties pastoral

[18] *Some Versions of Pastoral*, pp. 1 ff.

(considered as the only workable genre) became a potentially
revolutionary instrument, intimately concerned with the state of the
world and with the state of those who worried a lot about the state of
the world.

But the Terrors of the end time were at hand; and under this threat
some believed that more was required of them than Empson's
cautious 'contact with the worker'—something more sacrificial,
more ecstatic. A quiet contemplation of the working class in relation
to permanent truths of the sort Empson expounded was not enough.
There must be union, and the need for it was very urgent. Yet the
difficulties persisted: that lack of common intellectual interest
lamented by Auden, the fact that the company of middle-class
friends was more congenial than that of workers, except under
special and temporary circumstances, and the certainty that workers
could not be writers without ceasing to be workers.

One way of attacking this last assumption is to argue that it
depends on a limited and specialized view of value in writing. Forty
years on from Empson the Marxist critic Carole Snee tackles the
same subject. She doesn't even mention her upper-class predecessor,
through his position is the one she contests. She deplores the
unexamined confidence that there is something called Literature, the
production and valuation of which is reserved to the bourgeoisie,
even though one or two working-class people are allowed in by
special grace—Tressell, Grassic Gibbon, one or two more, perhaps.
And she insists that the dismantling of the bourgeois canon is a
necessary first step towards the establishment of working-class
writing as worth reading on its own terms. Confident that modern
Marxist literary theory has the means to deconstruct this insider/
outsider division, she nevertheless admits or complains that it has
not yet done so. Snee is not the first Marxist, by a long way, to
cogitate the peculiar dangers besetting proletarian fiction: the novel
is treacherous ground because of its largely bourgeois history, its
vested interest in the bourgeois shibboleth of 'individualism'. Yet
she believes that there are ways of using the suspect form without
being trapped by its ideology. She examines three Thirties working-
class writers as samples. Walter Greenwood's *Love on the Dole* (1933)
is condemned; it treats of the period 1922–31 without making
anything of the General Strike; it is individualistic, liberal,
bourgeois–romantic, short on political action, defeatist, inheriting
all the faults of the genre. But other writers show that these pitfalls

can be avoided. In his first novel, *The Means Test Man* (1937), Walter Brierley refused to allow the middle classes 'to appropriate working-class sensitivity'; unfortunately his next two books show a progressive deterioration: he succumbs to self-improvement and becomes an Author. However, there is Lewis Jones. In his two novels about the Welsh coalfield (*Cwmardy* (1937) and *We Live* (1939)) this miner–writer stays clear of liberal ideology. He contrives to present the collective life of Welsh miners and at the same time, or by the same token, draw 'characters who represent all the finest attributes of the working class, but who still live within these pages as people rather than cyphers'—thus solving the great problem of depicting collectivities in a form devised for the examination of individualities. Such faults as Jones commits Snee attributes to the lingering remnants of the novel's ancestry; after all, merely to find out what a novel *is* exposes the writer to that risk. And one book, *We Live*, is held to be triumphant over all handicaps. But of these three writers only Greenwood, as Snee points out, is accepted—and not with great enthusiasm—by the 'establishment'.[19]

In the Thirties the relation of the working class to literature was an urgent practical issue and not merely a problem of academic Marxist theory, as it is now. Edgell Rickword, for instance, said that what was needed (and in his view it was substantially achieved) was 'the drawing into the cultural ambit of a significant number of men and women who were barricaded out from participation in what was regarded as a middle-class preserve'. And he adds that the staff of the *Left Review* spent much time bringing working-class contributions up to scratch. For instance, James Hanley, reporting on a competition run by the paper in 1936, claimed to have judged it 'by Miltonic standards, clarity, simplicity, sensuousness. . . . I ruled out definitely propagandist matter.'[20] There may be some misunderstanding here of 'Miltonic standards', but it is obvious all the same that the intention was to open Literature, as the middle class understood the concept, to qualified aspirants from the working class—in short, to give that class access to what was known to be truly valuable. Hanley would not have understood Ms Snee; half a century on, it is quite

[19] C. Snee, 'Working-class Literature or Proletarian Writing?' in J. Clark, M. Heinemann, D. Margolies, and C. Snee (eds), *Culture and Crisis in Britain in the Thirties* (1979), 165–91. For more detailed comment on Lewis Jones, see Chapter 5.
[20] 'A Conversation with Edgell Rickword', *Review*, 11–12 (1965), 17–20.

usual to question the notion of value that then seemed obvious to 'educated' people, who knew about Milton, for example.

There was, however, a challenge to such assumptions, and it came from the Russian movement known as *proletcult*, which demanded a new start, a new literature of and for the proletariat, independent of the antecedent bourgeois literature. On the whole, though with different emphases, the most powerful Communist voices opposed this radical break with the past, and sought ways to prevent the abandonment of works formerly granted high value but tainted with pre-revolutionary ideologies. Trotsky held that the methods of art were independent of Marxism, arguing that this was a matter in which the Party need not interfere, though he wanted art to be made available to the masses. But in the circumstances non-intervention was too much to expect; what emerged from the deliberations of writers and from the Party was not an outright rejection of the past but a declaration, still requiring theoretical justification, that past literature could be put to Marxist uses. At the same time there emerged the doctrine of socialist realism which had such notable consequences for Soviet writing—and Soviet writers. There were some repercussions of this debate in the United States and England, but mostly rather weak ones.

Edmund Wilson's *Axel's Castle* (1931) was one of the first books to register the conflict between what is nowadays called 'the Modernist canon' and the now evident needs of socialism; it ends by calling for a break with the world of the private imagination and a new effort based on the example of Soviet Russia, 'a country where a central social–political idealism has been able to use and to inspire the artist as well as the engineer'. These words were actually written some years before 1934, when the Writers' Congress promulgated socialist realism. Wilson asks 'whether it is possible to make a practical success of human society, and whether, if we continue to fail, a few masterpieces, however profound or noble, will be able to make life worth living even for the few people in a position to enjoy them'—a question Walter Benjamin was also trying to answer.[21] Wilson was of course a bourgeois writer, and later the Party in America had some misgivings about using such people—indeed this was a great talking point at the time; but Herbert Gold stressed the importance of getting them into the John Reed Clubs, and wrote to an associate that

[21] E. Wilson, *Axel's Castle* (1931; 1959 edn.), 292–3.

'it should be very clear that no one is asked to change his mental habits. You believe in proletarian writing. Wilson believes in Proustian. I say bring him into the movement, if he is a writer of great influence and talent. We cannot afford to have aesthetic quarrels.'[22] But there were such quarrels, quickly merging with political differences. Some Communists feared that to admit writers such as Wilson would be to put proletarian writers at a disadvantage; the middle class should not be asked for help, but simply absorbed. Others believed that bohemian artists who had already abandoned their class could be brought into alliance with workers more directly involved in politics.

In England the Party welcomed some middle-class writers, but the relation was never an easy one. The whole issue came up quite suddenly, because of the remarkable lack of interest taken by middle-class intellectuals in politics up to the beginning of the Thirties. Auden is said never to have read a newspaper before 1930, Christopher Caudwell was quite apolitical until his sudden conversion to Communism in 1935; his Marxist books were written between that date and 1937, when he died in Spain. Such political *coups de foudre* lent an air of wildness and extremity to the subsequent remarks of the stricken.

I think that Arthur Calder-Marshall can once again give us an idea of the mood of the bourgeois convertites. He wrote a book called *The Changing Scene*, expressing strong distaste for the state of the nation in 1937 and expressing justifiable fears for its immediate future. In the world of books, he said, bourgeois individualism still flourished; indeed the vogue of psychoanalysis had induced bourgeois writers to turn inward even more than before. Their subjects had no general importance: 'Gerhardi, Michael Arlen, Rosamond Lehmann, all concentrated on a small clique of dilettantes with private incomes and an erotic itch that couldn't be satisfied.' Calder-Marshall goes on to divide writers into three camps:

those who openly advocated fascism, the most conspicuous of whom was Wyndham Lewis; those who still hoped that it was possible to maintain capitalism in this country without resort to fascism; and those who, understanding the political and economic situation in Europe, identified themselves with the working-class movement for international socialism.

[22] Quoted in D. Aaron, *Writers on the Left* (1961; 1977 edn.), 226.

This last was, of course, the writer's own party. Their programme was to foster, as the most characteristic development of the age, the growth of a proletarian literature. It would not be in the manner of Tressell; there would be no 'sloganism'. All that was needed was an objective account of capitalist society; justly rendered, it would condemn itself. Proletarian novels would not necessarily be written by proletarians (Calder-Marshall was soon to publish his own, *Pie in the Sky* (1937)) and they need not always be about strikes, demonstrations, and the distribution of pamphlets. They would, quite simply, represent the real world, seen from a revolutionary point of view.

In fact few of the writers he mentions as contributing to this new movement are working class: Ralph Bates, Christopher Isherwood, Storm Jameson, John Sommerfield, Leslie Halward, George Orwell, Naomi Mitchison. He does, with a certain desperation, give his approval to a play called *Where's that Bomb*, written collectively by London taxi-drivers. But for Calder-Marshall the main hope seemed to lie with the converted, the politically amorous bourgeois writer. He must give up the old, selfish middle-class idea that in writing he could or should 'express himself'; he must understand that his duty is to warn, to advise, to deliver urgent messages (as Auden famously put it, to 'make action urgent and its nature clear') and thus to serve the loved one, the beauty too little and too lately known, the proletariat.

All this suggests that, despite his commitment and enthusiasm, Calder-Marshall knew no better than anybody else what a revolutionary novel would look like, or what the literary function of the bourgeois sympathizer ought to be. Some such writers eventually came into contact with workers, either in routine work for the Party or in Spain. And Spain made action—including literary action —seem very urgent without necessarily making its nature clear. It has been pointed out that the three major books of early English Marxist criticism appeared in the first year of the Civil War. Two of them—Alick West's *Crisis and Criticism* and Ralph Fox's *The Novel and the People*—are now more or less forgotten (unjustly, I think). The third was Christopher Caudwell's *Illusion and Reality*, which is still read, but not much admired by modern Marxists.

Caudwell is in some ways an exemplary figure, a bourgeois writer of remarkable talent and industry whose acceptance of Communism really did have a religious quality. He became a rank-and-file Party worker in Poplar and then went to Spain, where he was killed in his first battle. He distinguishes very clearly between his beliefs and those of the 'bourgeois revolutionaries, anarchists who simply want the present state of things to end. . . . They still live in personal worlds,' he goes on, 'and imagine that the freedoms conferred by revolution will be bourgeois freedoms, which is why they bother so much about reports of censorship and interference with writers in the Soviet Union.'[23] This is the theme he develops at the end of his major work, *Illusion and Reality*. It is a demonstration of what love for the proletariat—vaguely aspired to by others—would really entail; a shade clinical, as no doubt Auden would have expected, but also requiring sacrifice, and, more than that, a psychic revolution in the lover. *Illusion and Reality* has plausibly been said to owe as much to Jung as to Marx.[24] Caudwell describes poetry as essentially collective, inseparable from the world of 'common emotion', and he thinks it deplorable that under capitalism it has grown ever more individualistic, private, and obscure. Nevertheless the Party should accept the help of the bourgeois anarchists, despite their being 'pathological and spiritually hysterical'; despite their erroneous belief that they could submit to the Party all save their art; despite their ability to see only the necessity, and not the beauty, of the post-revolutionary state. Despite all these crushing disadvantages they should be put to work, because anything that can help to destroy the existing system must be used. But there will be no turning back for such writers; unless they become truly proletarian their art will die. This full conversion will happen only when poetry is returned to the collectivity, when it is written for the million, as it is beginning to be in Russia.[25]

Caudwell, then, discriminates quite clearly between the convert and the flirt. He certainly hadn't solved all the problems. His own poetry he regarded as an expression of 'the inner world of feelings' which, he hoped, would be projected 'into the new world struggling to be born', a world which would have a new kind of poetry, the purpose of which would be to create 'new levels of sympathy' by raising Communist consciousness. He knew this poetry must not be propaganda merely; but how it would work—by a combination of

[23] C. Caudwell, *Romance and Realism* ed. S. Hynes (1970), 131–2.
[24] R. Curry, 'Christopher Caudwell: Marxist Illusion, Jungian Reality', *British Journal of Aesthetics*, 18 (1978), 291–9.
[25] *Illusion and Reality* (1938), 322–7.

Jungian and Communist collectivity of spirit—he perforce left vague.[26]

Caudwell thought of the relation between artist and worker as one of love—defined as 'the emotional element in social relations'. Trying to tell us the truth about love, he says it isn't what the movies suggest, nor is it what Freud thinks it is, or we should have a whole set of words to distinguish between sexual love, the love of friends, the love of one's children, the love of one's fellow humans. Sexuality is important because, via genetics, it creates consciousness, creates individuals; but even deeper than sex there is a primitive economics, which seems to be for Caudwell the deepest level of love. It emerges at different periods in the distorted forms imposed by economic history: chivalrous love in the feudal, passionate love in the bourgeois eras. In the present age, in the time of the death throes of capitalism, human relations lack even the distorted strength they had under feudalism; affection is conditioned by the cash economy, tenderness dies (a touch of D. H. Lawrence here), and love is displaced on to Fascist dictators. True social consciousness is repressed. Communism alone can restore direct contact with that primitive economic base and bring back love into human societies.[27] So love is collectivized, the otherness of the classes disappears, and Plato's halves unite again.

I've been emphasizing that the idea of love, in some phenomenal manifestation, was inseparable from the politics of left-wing bourgeois writers. To some it is the instrument of revolution, the agent of conversion; to others a more limited affair but still a rather alarming confrontation with the unknown, an extension of what one felt for one's friends to a whole class. Caudwell would have thought love for the Ideal Friend, or love for the foreign boy, trivial matters compared with the loving surrender to necessity required by Communism—a kind of loving which assumes the economic and psychic oneness of humanity, and which might well insist on your betraying your friend rather than your Party.

I suppose we could call Caudwell's declaration of love for the proletariat a version of pastoral. His desire for a consciousness so transformed reminds me of the lover possessed by the spirit of Tonka. The polite bohemian public schoolboys also had a pastoral vision of the workers, but, so to speak, also practised the pastourelle.

[26] Ibid. 137, 173.   [27] C. Caudwell, *Studies in a Dying Culture* (1938).

They thought they saw the necessity, but could not see its beauty. So Caudwell thought them failures, bourgeois anarchists of only temporary use. He was wrong, I think, despite their eventual defection; their experience was different from his, but it had its own value, and in their own ways they communicated that value, to which, in a sense, their failure contributed. It is impossible now to remember or to imagine the troubled bliss of left-wing life and thought in the Thirties, the fear and the guilt, but also the exultation of people who felt that upon them—the social misfits, the frivolous and 'consciously declassed minority', as Isherwood called his friends[28] —the ends of the earth had come. We have routinized apocalypse, but they sensed a once-for-all apocalypse as imminent.

There is a clear statement of the mood of the decade in the manifesto drawn up in 1932 by Edmund Wilson and his friends: 'The present crisis of the world . . . is something more than a mere crisis of politics and economics; and it will not pass with the depression. It is a crisis of human culture. What faces us today is the imperative need for new social forms, new values, a new human order.'[29] Or, as Auden said in a line he came later to detest, 'New styles of architecture, a change of heart.' If they failed to meet such a challenge, failure is exactly what, in such a situation, we have to expect. It is the quality of the failure we need to assess; and we need to ask in what degree it is our failure rather than theirs. But that is for another chapter.

[28] *Lions and Shadows* (1938; 1985 edn.), 152.
[29] *Letters on Literature and Politics, 1912–1972*, ed. E. Wilson (1977), 222.

3 · Mixed Feelings

THE crisis that engaged the minds and spirits of the bourgeois writers of the Thirties appeared to them to be unique; and in one respect at least it was so, for I do not think that any English writers before them—or since—have felt as they did about inequality and the absence of respect and affection between classes. There was an evident need for something more than fellow-feeling, more than progressive reform. It was not merely that they began to attend to the plight of the poor. They applied themselves to a need much more overwhelming—the inevitability of vast historical change, of revolution and war, of which poverty and class hatred were the social signs. Conscience was reinforced by intellect, and the desire to love one's fellow humans by fear.

Because of all this the Thirties offer us what we are not sure how to handle: a literature of conscience that is also a literature of fear, and sometimes of a certain pleasure in the fear, even of a wish to be clever about the fear and the pleasure.

> These years have seen a boom in sorrow;
> The presses of idleness issued more despair
>   And it was honoured;
> Gross Hunger took on more hands every month,
> Erecting here and everywhere his vast
>   Unnecessary workshops;
> Europe grew anxious about her health,
> Combines tottered, credits froze,
> And business shivered in a banker's winter . . .[1]

The years of slump see a boom in sorrow, despair is inflated as when too much money is printed, Hunger becomes an industrialist, a mass employer, when the normal mass employers are closing their factories and yards. These are conceited inversions—perhaps we might think them just a little too smart. But in the world of 1936 they were (and are) very telling. And this was one of the voices we listened to; it was Auden who found and formed the right period style. There were others who warned us of our spiritual desolation. Eliot was calling us

---

[1] *The English Auden*, ed. E. Mendelson (1977), 142.

'decent godless people' whose only monument would be 'the asphalt road | And a thousand lost golf balls'.[2] Ezra Pound blamed the bankers, 'news control and perverted publicity', and tried to sell his economic panacea.[3] John Strachey proved to the large Left Book Club readership that Communism was both desirable and inevitable. But a poet might believe that to be so, yet express, along with the excitement and alarm attending such a belief, a sense that the compound aura of feeling around it included also nostalgia and regret. It was hard to imagine the poetry of the future, and the poetry of the present had to deal with the particular sorrows and threats of the present, which required the sacrifice of much of the past to the necessities of history and conscience.

To understand what it felt like to be in this position we must first see that these writers were not simply experiencing one of those intermittent stirrings of conscience which had afflicted the intelligent bourgeoisie in the past, much as it does today. There really is a qualitative difference between these types of conscientious attention to social evils. Throughout the nineteenth century the attention of the well-to-do was at random intervals drawn to the existence of intolerable social conditions, and the harsh measures used to mitigate their consequences. When the crime rate increased greatly after the French Revolution those in power blamed the libertinism of that revolution, and took repressive countermeasures. But liberals blamed instead the policies of the government itself. 'Our progress towards the minimum of endurable privation', wrote William Maginn in 1830, 'has been as rapid as the most inveterate enemy of England could desire.' Prison turned occasional thieves into professional criminals; bankruptcy was common; and the principal remedy for these ills was emigration, either voluntary or compulsory, with consequent depletion of the labour force. The responsibility for social ills was firmly placed on the poor themselves.[4] The *Morning Chronicle* could startle its readers into a momentary awareness that the cities were really 'horrible muckheaps', as William Morris called them; Dickens could urge his readers to understand that rich and poor were of one body, that the diseases of the slums

---

[2] Chorus from 'The Rock', *Complete Poems and Plays, 1909–1950* (1952), 103.
[3] *Selected Prose*, ed. W. Cookson (1973), 249.
[4] 'The Desperate System: Poverty, Crime and Emigration', in *Fraser's Magazine* (July 1830) repr. in G. Levine (ed.), *The Emergence of Victorian Consciousness* (1967), 272–83.

were not obliged to spare the middle classes. Thackeray expressed his dismay at learning how people had to live in slums not five minutes away from his own Garrick Club. Mayhew's *Life and Labour of the London Poor* (1861–2) placed a lot of evidence, some of it horrible, some of it curious, before the public; and *The Economist* condemned his work as 'an encouragement to communism'.[5] But horror soon gave way to renewed indifference, and the problems were again left to the heroic charitable organizations, until the next wave of interest. These periodic alarms about the condition of England continued well into the present century, and they still go on. The uproar caused by the television play *Cathy Come Home* was typical: Tony Garnett told me that a year after its showing, when the urgent calls for action had subsided, the number of people in Cathy's position had greatly increased. No doubt it is now much larger.

Between these periodic awakenings many middle-class people appeared to resume their old view of poverty as inevitable or self-inflicted. The poor (the proletariat, as they began about this time to be called) were an anonymous unwashed mass, to be feared, despised, and disciplined. The severity with which they were treated by those forced into contact with them went far beyond what was needed to punish or even merely exploit them, as for example in heavy fines for lateness at work, and the prohibition of singing in factories.[6]

Most people rarely came into contact with the poor except in their capacity as servants. Engels, who had told the world about the lives of workers in Manchester, was impressed by the arrangements which made it unnecessary for the well-to-do ever to see the conditions under which those workers lived; the roads which carried them from their suburbs to their businesses were driven through the working-class districts in such a way that they did not need to pass through the mean streets. And he observed that 'the middle classes have more in common with every other nation in the world than with the proletariat which lives on their own doorsteps'.[7] Not the least remarkable aspect of this situation was the docility of the

[5] See G. Himmelfarb, 'The Culture of Poverty', in H. J. Dyos and Michael Wolff (eds), *The Victorian City* (1973), 707–36.

[6] See D. Craig, *The Real Foundations* (1974), 89–90.

[7] See S. Marcus, 'Reading the Illegible', in *The Victorian City* pp. 257–76; and F. Engels, *The Condition of the Working Class in England in 1844*, trans. and ed. W. O. Henderson and W. H. Challoner (1958).

working class. Engels saw that Chartism was simply too deferential in its manners, too gentle, to achieve its objectives. But he believed that the next slump in the cycle would inevitably produce a qualitative change, a change which entailed revolution; deference would stop, the attention of the middle class would no longer be switched on and off at convenient intervals; the bourgeoisie would be involved in a world-historical process, and not merely taking a look at the problem when it chose to do so.

He was wrong, of course, and his mistake was repeated in the Thirties, when capitalism was once again in its death throes, and history had again brought about that qualitative change which precedes revolution. But deference was again triumphing over tendencies to militancy. The conditions of the poor were perhaps not very different. The city was still the great image of social division, often not much changed from the previous century when Walter Bagehot, in a famous conceit that would nowadays qualify him as a Postmodernist, compared it to a newspaper: 'everything is there, and everything is disconnected;'[8] wealth and poverty, virtue and scandal, all in the same place. In the nineteenth century there was a popular song called 'I can't find Brummagem' and in the twentieth the middle-class poet Louis MacNeice, exiled there for a time, called it 'a sprawling inkblot', lived on its genteel south side, and escaped by car whenever he could, leaving behind his 'unresponsive' and 'undernourished' students; as they made the prison-like lecture-rooms resound to the verses of Homer recited in Midland accents they seemed as different from the 'clean-cut working man' of his fantasy as they were from Oxford undergraduates.[9] And 'up in the industrial district on the north side of Birmingham the air was a muddy pond and the voices of those who expected nothing a chorus of frogs for ever resenting and accepting the *status quo* of stagnation'.[10]

The calm or resignation of the proletariat in these pre-revolutionary times continued to puzzle middle-class left-wingers, and their puzzlement is a measure of the frightful task they set themselves when they proposed to breach the class frontier. I think again of Edmund Wilson's novel, in which the narrator begins to explain Marxism to his working-class mistress but soon gives up,

---

[8] Bagehot is admiring Dicken's talent for dealing with this disconnection. See P. Collins, 'Dickens and London', in *The Victorian City*, p. 34.
[9] Louis MacNeice, *The Strings are False* (1965), 130.   [10] Ibid. 135.

seeing that she can't believe it has anything to do with her and the way of life she knows and he doesn't. I myself lived through most of the Thirties in a small town in the Isle of Man which had very high seasonal unemployment. Poor children were easily identified because they wore clogs, issued free by the municipality to the children of the unemployed. These children were despised but also feared by those of us, not all that much richer, who wore boots or shoes, were brought up not to be rough like the clog-wearers, and threatened with their fate if naughty. There was some grumbling about the bosses when times were particularly hard, and even, at a moment of extreme poverty, a successful general strike. But for the most part the interests of working-class people didn't extend far beyond their own kind and their own problems. There was a good deal of gaiety and gossip, since within these limits everybody knew everybody else, or if not, knew her cousin. There was no great envy or dislike of the gentry, indeed there was a measure of respect (one was always being told to behave like a gentleman). Animosity was reserved largely for those who were a rung lower, the wearers of clogs. I don't remember any talk of revolution and the word 'bourgeosie' wasn't used; nor, for that matter, was 'proletariat'.

All this tended to reduce the possibility of concerted proletarian action; it was just the sort of thing the infatuated bourgeois intellectual couldn't know about. There was another consideration tending to reduce that possibility, no doubt less surprising to us than to people in the Thirties, few of whom will have known about it anyway (which illustrates the difference between living in a period and knowing about it later). It is this: people who had work were better off than ever before; real wages rose throughout the decade, and the gap between those in work and the unemployed steadily widened. It was no easier then than now to feel the misfortunes of others; and as one motored down the new asphalt roads to the ball-strewn golf course the unfortunate, like Engels's slum-dwellers, were nowhere to be seen, and were remembered, if at all, only for their feckless refusal to prosper. Yet there was a myriad of them, out of sight, not only of the poor but of the crippled. More than two-and-a-half million men were drawing pensions for disabilities sustained in the still quite recent war. These were carefully apportioned: 16s. for a whole right arm, 14s. for an arm missing below the elbow, and so on. These men tended to show up only on Armistice Day. And if you had £5 a week, poverty and privation were remote considerations. If you were a 'rentier poet' with £500 a year you thought about them only because of a deliberate and educated act of conscience. And once committed to this course you might feel compassion, beyond necessity no doubt, for almost the whole population; manual workers earned about £3 a week, and 88 per cent of the population had less than £250 a year.[11] It is true that a family like my own managed fairly well on £3, and people lived with enviable style on £5. But the bourgeois poets could hardly be expected to know that.

The point is that consciousness of the need and the possibility of action was to a very considerable extent an affair of the middle-class conscience. And it is surely to the credit of the intellectual left, now somewhat despised for *naïveté*, that they were so moved, that they came to believe that they must do something about the whole system that in their view made poverty and war equally inevitable. When they joined the Communist Party, or fellow-travelled, they were not climbing on to a bandwagon; even in the days of its greatest pre-war success, the great days of the Left Book Club, before the German–Soviet Pact, the Party had only a few thousand members. Ordinary people only began to worry about world politics in 1938, with the frantic trench-digging in Hyde Park, and the barrage balloons, so weird then, soon to be so familiar. Moreover the events of 1939, including the introduction of conscription, made political argument an irrelevance, especially for nineteen-year-olds like myself. Even those who had said they would not fight in a capitalist–imperialist war quietly went along. The rhetoric of the coming proletarian revolution was no longer much heard.

As I've suggested, it had always been in some degree ignorant. The proletariat wasn't the beautiful, doomed, unlucky, but potentially irresistible body fantasized by the bourgeois Communist sympathizer, transferring his sense of what it meant to be outcast, alienated, *maudit*, to the worker. The proletariat was a strange tribe, and it might be lovable. In fact intellectuals invented Mass Observation to find how the workers lived and behaved, much as if they were a 'primitive' tribe and the Observers anthropologists willing to learn a new language in return for knowledge of an alien culture.

[11] I take these figures from J. Stevenson, *British Society, 1914–1945*, (1984). In P. Hamilton, *Hangover Square* (1941) – a novel which scrupulously registers the conditions of life immediately before the war – a meal for two at a very expensive London restaurant, together with a great deal to drink, costs £2. 13s. 7d.

They observed such events as the Silver Jubilee celebrations of George V and the coronation of George VI, and they observed perfectly ordinary, arbitrarily chosen days like 12 May 1937. They wanted to know what people did in dance-halls, bathrooms, and pubs. They developed the fashionable genre of reportage, and they unwittingly established techniques of market research that are still too much with us. Their motives were excellent; they wished to learn about and possibly love the unknown, the Other.

The poets looked at the proletariat less methodically, more speculatively than the Mass Observers. Tending to repeat one another, they were, for example, astonished at the degree to which the poor seemed to depend for comfort on the cinema—not Russian films or John Grierson's, but Hollywood's.

> Enter the dream-house, brothers and sisters, leaving
>   Your debts asleep, your history at the door;
>   This is the home for heroes, and this loving
>   Darkness a fur you can afford . . .
>
> Bathed in this common source, you gape incurious
>   At what your active hours have willed—
>   Sleepwalking on that silver wall, the furious
>   Sick shapes and pregnant fancies of your world.[12]

How did Cecil Day-Lewis know this? He didn't; he assumed it must be so. And where did George Barker find the word 'marvellous' used as he uses it in these lines?

> I encountered the crowd returning from amusements,
>   The Bournemouth Pavilion, or the marvellous gardens,
>   The Palace of Solace, the Empyrean Cinema . . .[13]

Here 'marvellous' means, roughly, 'not marvellous', or 'what ordinary people ignorantly think marvellous', and Barker of course got it from Auden ('long marvellous letters', etc.). It may also have been Auden who first put it about that cinemas were a pathetic kind of solace for the poor: 'bowers of bliss | Where thousands are holding hands', 'Gaumont theatres | Where fancy plays on hunger to produce | The noble robber, ideal of boys.'[14] It didn't matter if you used the cinema yourself as a means of escape, as MacNeice and his wife did, four or five times a week, in Birmingham, going

---

[12] Cecil Day-Lewis, in *Poetry of the Thirties*, ed. Robin Skelton (1964), 69.
[13] Ibid. 186.   [14] *The English Auden*, p. 142.

solely for entertainment and never for value, holding hands like a shopgirl with her boy-friend. The organist would come up through the floor, a purple spotlight on his brilliantined head, and play us the 'Londonderry Air' and bow and go back to the tomb. Then the stars would return and the huge Cupid's bows of their mouths would swallow up everybody's troubles—there were no more offices or factories or shops, no more bosses or foremen, no more unemployment and no more employment, no more danger of disease or babies, nothing but bliss in a celluloid world where the roses are always red and the Danube is always blue.[15]

You can tell from the tone that it was all the other people in the cinema who were experiencing this bogus solace and not the Mac-Neices, who were there with them, but not of them, almost nightly, being entertained, not seeking value where only the others could be deluded into thinking they might find it.

Such, it was supposed, were the compensations of terribly restricted lives. Here another poet describes how those poor lives are lived:

> The greengrocer's cart, the haggling to save a halfpenny,
> On the boiled orange or the Argus-eyes potato;
> The fecund red-elbowed women with their baskets,
>   And their humourless menfolk.
>
> These will never hold aces or travel farther
> Than a tram will take them. And their summum bonum
> The threepenny double which comes up by a head,
>   Unlimited bitter.[16]

Those lines come from a long poem, desperate, indignant, compassionate; but it certainly makes the poor keep their distance. The Horatian stanza is itself a mark of detachment, even of retreat. Then there is the learned little joke about the potatoes, the patronizing *summum bonum*, the women so very unlike our own ('fecund red-elbowed') and their men, so very unlike us ('humourless'). The workers' Cockaigne is defined by a bet won with a derisory stake, and a gutter flowing with beer. The poem is saying to the poor what Upward's hero said to his girl: 'How ugly you are!' But it is also trying to add, 'This is what we must learn to love.' Those fashionable definite articles (the cart, the haggling, the orange, the potato, the women, the threepenny double), also from Auden (neatly labelled by David Trotter, who calls them articles of 'unfulfilled

[15] *The Strings are False*, p. 138.   [16] K. Allott, *Collected Poems* (1975), 17.

specificity'[17]), mean *ex uno disce omnes*: from these types you will understand the collective whole. I don't know about boiled oranges, which sound exotic, but the proximity of this one to the obviously substandard potato suggests that it represents the exoticism of a poverty we do not, at this stage anyway, share.

Kenneth Allott's poem goes on to tell us that the poet lies in bed thinking of these things, hearing the water knocking in the pipes, or perhaps it is his own heart; while outside the 'necessary' light awakens 'the seasons and cities'. The light is necessary as Auden's lovers are necessary, part of the going on of a world from which the poet contemplates his detachment. 'The moon is usual. . . . The planets rush towards Lyra in the lion's charge . . . And tomorrow comes. It's a world. It's a way.'[18] The usual is given cosmic scope, yet we don't belong to it. Mere rags of it as we are, we cannot fail to join the universe; yet to make a point of our having to do so also sets us apart, just as we are apart from the red-elbowed women and the humourless men whom we must also somehow join. To know the ordinary other one is forced to be extraordinary, which makes it difficult to join the ordinary. The poetry emerges as at once cool and distraught, and so much in the fashion and dialect of the time that to see its value requires a patient effort of historical understanding. Given that, we may read it not exactly as it was but with a supplement of later sympathy which shows it to be struggling for a cathexis unwillingly willed. It is an attempt to do as Auden's sages taught—to renounce 'what our vanity has chosen', to pursue 'understanding with patience like a sex'.

The sheer difficulty of pursuing understanding like a sex was coldly described by George Orwell as both moral and technical.

Books about ordinary people behaving in an ordinary manner are extremely rare [he said], because they can only be written by someone who is capable of standing both inside and outside the ordinary man, as Joyce for instance stands inside and outside Bloom; but this involves admitting to yourself that you *are* an ordinary person for nine-tenths of the time, which is exactly what no intellectual ever wants to do.[19]

But, even if being a writer is to be truly extraordinary only one-tenth of the time, you are a writer when you are writing, and so extra-

[17] D. Trotter, *The Making of the Reader* (1984), 113.
[18] *The English Auden*, pp. 165–6.
[19] G. Orwell, *Collected Essays, Journalism and Letters*, ed. S. Orwell and I. Angus (1968), i. 230, written in August 1936.

ordinary, even when writing about the ordinary, the necessary, the usual; and Joyce would serve equally well as evidence in support of this truism. Orwell himself was compelled to behave in an extraordinary way, to be a writer of pastoral, by the excitements of those early days in Barcelona, intimations of proletarian triumph which for a moment induced even in Auden a sense of solidarity with the workers. Orwell's essay 'Looking back on the Spanish War' ends with a poem about an Italian militiaman, 'his battered face | Purer than any woman's', and about a handshake that is as much between classes as between men:

> The strong hand and the subtle hand
> Whose palms are only able
> To meet within the sound of guns . . .[20]

So to Orwell himself it seemed that the writer must search for and love an ordinary wisdom different from his own (the Italian soldier 'was born knowing what I had learned | Out of books and slowly'); and there is no inaccuracy here in using the word 'love' and no difficulty in understanding what it was that Orwell loved—a person who stood for a class:

a fierce, pathetic, innocent face . . . which I only saw for a minute or two . . . He symbolizes for me the flower of the European working class, harried by the police of all countries, the people who fill the mass graves of the Spanish battlefields and are now, to the tune of several millions, rotting in forced-labour camps.

He is one soldier but all that as well:

> . . . the thing I saw in your face
> No power can disinherit:
> No bomb that ever burst
> Shatters the crystal spirit.

Orwell didn't often write like that; but that he did so on this occasion shows the special quality of the intellectual's attitude to the worker, however difficult it was to articulate. It isn't the slight ache of conscience over breakfast; it isn't anything Morris or Ruskin or Shaw would have felt. It is also very different from that 'aesthetic'

---

[20] *Homage to Catalonia.* (The Penguin edn. of 1966, etc. reprints the essay and the poem, pp. 246–7; they originally appeared in *England Your England* in 1953, but are dated 1943 by the author.)

form of socialism to which Wilde gave his blessing, a socialism that did not seek the handclasp of subtle with strong, but hoped by a redistribution of income and property to avoid such contacts altogether. 'The chief advantage of Socialism is undoubtedly the fact that Socialism would relieve us from that necessity of living for others which, in the present condition of things, presses so hard on nearly everybody.' Hideous poverty, hideous ugliness, hideous starvation, says Wilde, tempt one to try to ameliorate things, which always makes them worse. Despite its facetious tone, Wilde's essay encapsulates some of the stronger motives of English parlour socialism. The sentiments of the Thirties writers were different because they wanted, or tried to want, that handclasp with the unknown and innocent oppressed.

It is part of the story that the wish to love was accompanied by its opposite, an uneasy desire to withdraw, a repugnance like that of Upward's hero. Stephen Spender explained that in the end he finally had no real choice but to prefer his own aesthetic individualism to the 'historically correct position'.

To believe that my individual freedom could gain strength from my seeking to identify myself with 'progressive' forces was different from believing that my life must become an instrument of means decided upon by political leaders. I came to see that within the struggle for a juster world there is a further struggle between the individual who cares for long-term values and those who are willing to use any and every means to gain their political ends—even good ends. Within even a good social cause, there is a duty to fight for the pre-eminence of individual conscience . . . the individual must not be swallowed up by the concept of social man.[21]

Spender is thinking of the disillusioning tactics of the Party in those years, but the word that keeps on recurring is 'individual', and the sacrifice that is refused is the sacrifice of individuality, of the subtle hand; once the position is clearly understood, the writer, unless he is as totally committed as Caudwell or Upward, simply backs away from proletarianization; the sacrifice is too appalling, he feels he would have nothing left to work with or indeed to love with.

So most of the middle-class writers did fall away from active leftist politics as the decade drew towards its end. But the record of their affair with the workers is an honourable one, and we shouldn't allow

[21] S. Spender, *World within World* (1951; 1956 edn.), 311–12.

stock responses about pink or pansy poets to usurp our judgement. They had mixed feelings, but, as Auden remarked, poetry 'might be defined as the clear expression of mixed feelings',[22] which could very well consist of a consciousness of extraordinary novelty and deep anxieties about loving the unknown.

A clear expression of similarly mixed feelings is Edward Upward's *The Spiral Ascent*, a trilogy of novels long meditated and completed only in 1977. It has won less attention than it deserves, perhaps because it came so late, perhaps because it was easy to deplore Upward's departure from the manner of his admired early story 'The Railway Accident', which, as Isherwood records in *Lions and Shadows*, was one of the Mortmere fantasies devised by Upward and Isherwood in their time at Cambridge. There is also a change of manner from Upward's early novel *Journey to the Border* (1938). Samuel Hynes, in one of his rare mistaken judgements, says that 'the tension between his imagination and his political ideology shrivelled his natural gifts, and left him an arid, unimaginative and unreadable realist'.[23] In fact Upward did feel he had to achieve a new socialist simplicity of style, but he believed he could do so without ceasing to be an artist; for 'an artist cannot give his best to a political cause if in his art he is a politician first and an artist second'. Of course it was difficult to hold this position, and indeed holding it is a principal subject of his book. He could not altogether abandon the style of fantasy which came naturally to him as a writer; but, although it is true that the first volume of the trilogy represents a willed socialist-realism, Upward can justifiably claim that in the rest of the work he was moving to something richer—not the old Balzac bottles with new wine in them, but what he calls 'new forms'. He admits that he found this progress easier after he became disillusioned with politics —'the Party, I was able to see, was becoming un-Marxist'—and when he left the Party in 1948 he was in a position to abandon the strict canons of socialist realism, or to transform that kind of realism in very remarkable ways.[24]

Upward's hero is a middle-class, public-school poet, sure of his vocation but full of what Caudwell would have described as an anarchistic hatred of his own class, of the 'poshocrats' as he always

---

[22] W. H. Auden, *New Year Letter* (1941), 119.
[23] S. Hynes, *The Auden Generation* (1976), 317.
[24] 'Conversation with Edward Upward', *Review*, 11–12 (1965), 65–7.

calls them. The early scenes report with remarkable directness some naïve conversations between this poet, who is a straight version of Upward himself, and his friend, who is Isherwood. '"I've realized lately that I'm against the plus-foured plutocracy, and for the cockneys and lower orders,"' says the Isherwood character. '"I'm for them too," Alan said. "But I haven't your courage. I am afraid they will despise me. How did you do it?" "By behaving naturally. They are rather proud of their gentlemanly friend."' These lower orders are contrasted with the guests at the big holiday hotel, blazered young men and confidently striding girls. 'In their dress, their voices, their every minutest gesture and facial movement, they represented for Alan what he loathed more than anything else in the world: they were the loyal young supporters of that power . . . which despised the living poets and the truth.' Not long after this, however, Alan goes to bed with one of the confidently striding girls; she is about to be married but clearly enjoys her bourgeois irresponsibility. The theorists were always saying that all socialist realism need do to discredit the bourgeoisie is to show it as it actually is.

As one reads these early pages it is difficult to avoid the thought that this very deliberate attempt to invent a Communist style of writing merely proves that the new style is bound to be mistaken for bad writing by the unreconstructed bourgeoisie. However, Upward, even in this first volume, confounds this judgement by doing some good bourgeois writing, too. Certainly the effect is original, and it seems to me that the value of the whole is enhanced by the intrusion of this highly accented unproletarian rhetoric into flat grey stretches of candid socialist realism. In the representation of natural objects for instance, Upward cannot prevent himself from writing well in an older style: 'Then the miniature waves detaching themselves from the spent breaker and scarcely having the power of individual motion: these flopped on the sand with pause and dip like the rolling of a metal ellipse, or like the movement of the genitals of a naked male runner.' For all its ideological assertiveness, its continual worrying about how to mix solitary art and comradely Party business, Upward's book is always *written*, always organized, and always true to the sort of self-consciousness that is supposed to be the privilege of the privileged. In that degree it is pastoral, but it does not acquiesce in the fate of the poor. And if it was true, as Upward believed in 1937, that only a Marxist or near-Marxist attitude could produce good writing,[25] it was equally true, and just as well understood by him, that only good *writers* could produce good writing, and that, because of their traditional habits of mind and of work, good writers would have their difficulties with Communism, and find it hard to avoid pastoral attitudes to the workers.

Here Alan and his friends are watching some workers at a dance: ' "What is it that makes them so fine?" . . . "It can't be just sex." "No. Perhaps it's beauty, eh?" "Then it's because they're *living*." "Yes, that's partly it. But there's more to it than that . . . I've got it . . . It's because they're doomed." "Boy, I believe you're right." "It's because in ten to fifteen years' time all these girls will be prematurely middle-aged and ugly. And they're dancing now in defiance of the inevitable rot which will come upon them." "Yes, that's it." ' Later this insight is developed: it isn't only the young women who are doomed; the men are just as fine and they're doomed, too. ' "What makes people vile is being comfortably off. That's why most of the hotel visitors are so poisonous. They are the wicked, the devils. Only the doomed are good, and we must be on their side always." ' His friend agrees. ' "Our duty is to live among the doomed, and in our poetry we must record and celebrate what they are." ' And then Alan names the price to be paid for choosing the noble and rejecting the vile: ' "We ourselves, in our own way, are doomed too . . . We shall always be misfits, not properly belonging to any social class. We shall never settle down anywhere. We must walk the earth. We must descend into hell." '

There is often a certain quasi-religious fervour in Upward, but rarely to the degree that in this passage he attributes to himself as a young man: first to be like the disciples and walk the earth, homeless and without possessions; then to be like Christ and harrow hell. It seems to be weirdly excessive, absolutely dated, yet because rather than in spite of that, it sounds right. It would be as well to add that there is present also a hint of self-irony, a suggestion of reserve. And we can't grasp the full sense of these opening pages until their material reappears, splendidly transformed, at the close of the trilogy, 760 pages later.

What follows it more immediately is Alan's going to bed with his girl poshocrat, and then contemplating suicide. He understands that

[25] 'Sketch for a Marxist Interpretation of Literature', in C. Day-Lewis (ed.), *The Mind in Chains* (1937), 48.

a commitment to Communism could save him, but fears the effect of such a move on his writing. His poetry had failed hitherto because it wasn't, for want of such commitment, rooted in life and reality. To have any hope of writing well he must join the Party. But he must not do so simply in order to be able to write poetry. And in any case Party work might prevent his writing. Finally he joins because there is no tolerable alternative.

When Alan meets the workers at the local branch he is struck by the drabness of the habitat and the beauty of the inhabitants: 'From their eyes, bleared or bright or set in undernourished faces marked with skin disease, there looked out the life of the future.' They were finer than the well-dressed men and women from the hotel, more beautiful than the well-kept girl he had fallen in love with in the last days of his bourgeois life. He must work with these people, distribute pamphlets, turn up at meetings; he must also write, but there could be no compromise with bohemianism or liberal anarchism. Shunning bourgeois romance, he takes up with Elsie, who is plain and has not 'the look of a lady'; when he marries her he is quite expressly 'marrying the party'. She is thus a perfect emblem of the sexualized politics I've been trying to explain.

There is no salvation outside the Party, but we are not allowed to forget that its routine apocalyptic certainties, ritual condemnations, and repetitive propaganda can be tedious. Nevertheless the faith, as expounded in Alan's 'dusty stable loft', will prevail, and it is a great thing to be living at this hour of crisis, 'qualitatively different from former periodic crises'. The hour which should have struck in 1917—when the clock was stopped by the interventions of democratic socialism, by a Labour Party which was merely an instrument of capitalism—that hour is now at hand.

Writing after the event, Upward must have been conscious of historical ironies. The Labour Party ceased to be the servile instrument of capital when Moscow, in the interest of the Popular Front, suddenly said it wasn't. The confident assertion that 'Communism was the only force in the world which was uncompromisingly on the side of the doomed and against them who wanted to keep them doomed' must surely have acquired an ironical ring after the Stalinist purges became common knowledge. But at this stage Alan is keeping faith with a pure Communism that can cohabit with poetry. He is aware of a tension between them, but that tension is exactly what must be resolved by faith and works.

The beauty of Upward's slowly developing design is that such conflicts are registered and reconciled, as perhaps they only could be reconciled, in a work of art. It may be that in this respect it stands alone. Some of Upward's younger contemporaries thought their duty to be the writing of articles and pamphlets or poems about those who excelled all others at the making of driving-belts, thereby violating their sense of what poetry really was. Upward finds a way of putting in all the pedestrian detail and giving it a relation to the whole work (a criterion of value despised, I'm afraid, by modern Marxists). Alan finishes his long poem after many years of work, and his poem is Upward's novel, with all its longueurs and embarrassments. Here is a hero who is disgusted by Party rhetoric, by the stereotyped gesture, even by the infidelity of its leaders to Marxist Leninism; yet when he is expelled from the Party he falls ill with the sickness of the excommunicated.

Upward calls his trilogy 'a dialectical triad'—the political and the poetic as dialectical opposites, with a synthesis at the end, following the 'spiral ascent'. The final volume represents the synthesis. Alan is no longer described in the third person; the narrator is now 'I'. He has withdrawn into bourgeois security, but in finishing the book he simultaneously finishes his poem, so that they share a beautiful coda, the effect of which is to synthesize poetry and Communism.

To express admiration for such refined structures and transformations is to use measures devised for the sort of writing which advocates of proletarian novel reject. However, they are the measures appropriate to such skill and originality. Anybody who wants quick assurances that these are the proper terms of praise might look at a recent short story of Upward's, called 'At the Ferry Inn', which appeared in 1985[26] and will shortly form part of a new collection. It recounts a single incident and is seemingly a quite flat and over-detailed piece of slightly disguised autobiography. On inspection, however, it is not that at all. A poet called Walter Selwyn, quite obviously Auden, pays a visit to his old friend Arnold Olney, that is Upward, on the Isle of Wight, where Upward happens to live. They have been estranged for forty years (perhaps since Auden's departure to the United States in 1939). The ferry will bring Selwyn over for a day before he returns to New York. The arrival of the ferry is described with much detail. Among its passengers Olney observes a

[26] *London Magazine* (July 1985), 3-13.

young man, 'tall, broad-hipped, sloping-shouldered', his hair thick
and yellow, his cheeks plump and smooth-skinned. It is as if only a
week or two has passed since their last meeting.

Olney (Upward) has had a dream about his friend in which he met
him at the ferry, remembering at the same time Auden's sonnet 'just
as·his dream foretold—which, though he doesn't say so, contains
the lines 'at each meeting, he was forced to learn, | The same mis-
understanding would arise . . .' 'How well Auden's sonnet gets
the inconsequent feeling of dream,' thinks Olney. In the dream
the poet's face is 'saggingly old'. Also in the dream Olney
accepts a suitcase from a stranger, and places it on the steps of a
bank.

The friends drink at the Ferry Inn, with a group of hostile
blue-blazered poshocrats at the bar. Perhaps they overheard Olney
telling his friend about the bomb in the dream, and the interpretation
offered by Selwyn, which is that the bomb stands for the dreamer's
guilt for so many years of political activism. 'You were loyal for
longer than the rest of us', says the poet, 'to the "clever hopes", as
Auden afterwards called them, that we all fell for in the nineteen
thirties, but your book has brilliantly rejected them at last.' He has
been reading the final volume of *The Spiral Ascent* (which actually
came out four years after Auden's death). The author of that book
protests that he was 'deconverted' not from Communism but from
Stalinism. But the poet insists on congratulating him for having
understood that he must put his trust not in politicians but in artists.
'Art', he says, quoting Baudelaire in an Anglo-American French
accent, 'is the best testimony human beings can give of their dignity.'
By now they sense the growing disapproval of the blazered poshocrats; but the author nevertheless affirms his confidence in Leninist
Marxism as a force in a world of deepening capitalist crisis; the
coming revolution must prevent nuclear war. The poet now says
that a proletarian revolution was never a clever hope, adding that
poets didn't save a single Jew from the gas chambers. Whereupon he
departs to the lavatory, leaving his host to reflect on the hostility of
the yachtsmen, but also to remember that, had he not known the
poet, he 'would never have known how marvellous human life at its
best could be'. After a long wait he goes in search of his friend,
fearing that he might have fallen ill or been beaten up. But he has
gone, and Olney can only glimpse him on the disappearing ferry, his
face 'even more saggingly and horrifyingly old' than it had been in

the dream. Was the poet offended? No; he had waved cheerfully, the estrangement was over, though they could never meet again.

It is a complex tale, dream within dream; here is a dreamlike double Auden, quoting himself as if he were another poet, the old poet quoting the young one, of whom he no longer approves; here is Upward's paranoid vision of middle-class manners. The inn of the outer dream is the womb towards which, on such occasions, there is a retreat. The poet's face is old in the dream, young in the dreamed reality. There is a synthesis of old aspirations and old conflicts, the clever hopes raised above cleverness, the Thirties as the low dishonest decade of the defector, the very poet who had, in that time, shown how marvellous human life could be. Reportage and fantasy are reconciled. Baudelaire was right; but so, too, was Marx; and so too was Kafka in his union of world and dream.

Upward is sometimes called naïve, or even ignorant, but to join that chorus is to accept the myth which, as I've said, is partly the creation of Orwell, though it also owes much to political opponents like Wyndham Lewis. From Lewis we get an antithetical view of Thirties politics, as well as of human dignity. He doesn't want to love the proletariat—the peons, the *Massenmenschen*—and he does not love those who wish to love them; they earn his contempt and disgust as bad artists. If Lewis wasn't interested in peons he wasn't interested, either, in bourgeois individuals. His characters tend to be types, humours, even marionettes.

The Thirties pamphleteering of Lewis, 'that lonely old volcano of the right' as Auden almost affectionately called him,[27] is pretty well forgotten, but *Hitler* (1931), *Left Wings over Europe* (1936), and *Count Your Dead* (1937) were of some importance in their day. Lewis's latest biographer calls *Hitler* 'scantily researched and hastily written' —he hadn't even read *Mein Kampf*—but it was less a plug for Hitler than an expression of his hatred of Weimar, homosexuality, and the English writers who liked both.[28] Its contempt for the masses is so virulent that the Marxist critic Fredric Jameson, by ingenious dialectical manœuvres, can argue that its 'oppositional stance' puts the book finally on the side of the revolution.[29] Nobody except biographers and historians would want to read it now, and even Lewis's belated recantations (*The Jews, are they Human?* and *The Hitler Cult*

---

[27] 'Letter to Lord Byron', Part V, in *The English Auden*, p. 198.
[28] J. Meyers, *The Enemy: A Biography of Wyndham Lewis* (1980), 190.
[29] F. Jameson, *Fables of Aggression* (1979), 179 ff.

(both 1939)) have no interest; but *The Revenge for Love* is sometimes called the finest political novel of its time.

Lewis's novel appeared in 1937, at a time when left-wing writers were most deeply involved in the Republican cause, and it was read as an anti-Communist manifesto. So in a way it was; but Communist is for Lewis but one fraud in a world of frauds. To be a Communist is to be either a hired hand or a victim. What makes Lewis's position idiosyncratic is that he sees the sordor of the world of Communism as analogous to that of bogus art. Day-Lewis's confession that he felt small when he saw a Communist is repeatedly and derisively cited as evidence that a fake will always feel small when confronted with the real thing, however ugly. Lewis's Communist agent, Percy Hardcaster, is not a political idealist but a technician: 'There is a *technique* of the general strike, of agitation, of the *coup d'état*. Those are technical problems. Once you begin *acting* instead of merely talking, you become a technician.' Hardcaster accepts as part of his business both the beatings he suffers and the amateurish stupidity of his middle-class associates, just as the real artist, Lewis, accepts the rough treatment he gets from frauds and philistines, and the amateurish pseudo-artists that surround him. Communism and the business of forging paintings have exactly the same moral status.

So Percy gets some ironical respect because he is a professional; the real villains are the middle-class intellectuals. In fact they are the only real Communists because Communism is a fraud and only frauds would profess to believe in it; Percy at least isn't a fraud, nor are the worker-Communists, who are in it for what they can get. The workman, when he becomes a Communist,

regards it as just another job—a jolly sight better paid than any he can get out of the bosses. And when he makes himself into a Communist he brings with him all his working-class cynicism, all his underdog cowardice and disbelief in everything and everybody. . . . That is why Marx insisted on the necessity of his *hatred* being exploited.

When a middle-class intellectual argues that his purpose is to free the workers from such moral bondage, he is given an unsavoury account of proletarian manners and told derisively, 'It is with *that* that you have got to make your Communism rhyme.' The person who wants to free the workers is, significantly, a painter of abstracts. 'Don't you ever see anything—except *abstractions*? Like your pictures! But you are dealing with men and women of flesh and blood.

A mob of treacherous idiots! That's what you're doing—who snigger up their sleeves at you for the sucker you are . . .'[30]

Here, then, is the opposition, in the form of a book about Spain which consigns the Republican cause to the hands of mercenaries, dupes, and frauds, and is especially hard on worker-loving pink artists of the sort I've been praising. But Lewis's contempt for them, and for the workers, is really only a special case of his disgust with the human world in general. His novel has two central emblems: a grotesque dwarf and a malignantly howling baby. They stand for what forces Lewis into his role as Enemy—the repulsiveness of human generation, of a race malformed, bitter, and loathsome. Much the same spirit informs his hatred of homosexuality (which he rather oddly supposed to be a consequence of the unfairness to men of bourgeois marriage laws[31])—like Communism it was a fraudulent cult, but he saw these cults as having the malignant, distorted energy of the dwarf and the baby. Admirers of Lewis tend, I think, to smooth him out, to ignore the deeper sources of his disgust, as I think Julian Symons does in his introduction to the 1962 edition of *The Revenge for Love.* He treats the book as a justified attack on 'parlour Communists' and on the 'the liberal myth about Communist behaviour', a myth we can all now see through because we know 'about the honeycomb of deceit and treachery that marked every Communist Party in the Stalinist era'. Symons reports with irony Lewis's expressed hope that 'his book would some day be read as a novel, with its politics forgotten'; in his view it earns its status as one of the three great political novels of the century (the others being *The Middle of the Journey* (1947) and *Darkness at Noon* (1940)) precisely because of the energy with which it exposed the liberal myth.[32] These are all remarkable books, I admit, but their value cannot be dependent on the myth that they are good because they expose a myth. It is not enough to have seen through something, and Lewis knew that, was aware that opinions quite different from his own could be incorporated in works of art. Upward's achievement, for instance, seems to me quite untouched by Lewis's polemic. And both his novel and Lewis's have what is more important than a critique of political attitudes in a past age: they surprise us by their

[30] W. Lewis, *The Revenge for Love* (1937; 1962 edn.), 210, 206, 225–6.
[31] W. Lewis, *The Diabolical Principle* (1931), 146.
[32] Introduction to *The Revenge for Love* (1962), vii–xvi.

own complexity, and by the force with which they violate common-place perceptions, whether out of hatred for the self-seeking, de-formed, brutal, and rank-scented mass of humanity, or out of love for the doomed and a desire to redeem them.

There are other myths as unacceptable as the one Symons is glad to have seen demolished. There is the myth of the uncorrupted classless artist facing alone the plebeian mob, its slippery tribunes and its deluded soft collaborators, the phoney artists and the sentimental intellectuals. And whether or no we accept Lewis in this Coriolanus pose—some do and some do not—it seems that his indictment of the intellectual left has to a large extent prevailed. There is a willingness to believe that the work of these writers was founded on ignorance (Orwell's repeated charge) or on bad faith and stupidity (Lewis's repeated charge). And there is an implication that to reject the politics of the bourgeois left of the Thirties implies the necessity to reject its art. Which accounts for our over-willingness to accept harsh judgements, sometimes made by the writers themselves, of a literature that might still, if we could escape from this myth, strike us as bold and troubling.

I don't hope to show that these writers were never deluded, never silly; nor that their courtship of the proletariat did not lead them into difficulties and out of their depths. But we should not allow our opinion of their politics to serve as a judgement on their art. Indeed one only has to say so out loud for the point to be over-obvious. If I were referring to the great moderns of the previous generation—to Yeats, Pound, Eliot—the remark would be thought a truism; yet that elementary wisdom doesn't at present come into play when we are talking about the Thirties. Perhaps the difficulty is that we are still in some ways close to the writers of the Thirties, some of them still alive, so that it is in that measure harder to think about them without confusing history and value, without allowing our disillu-sion with their politics to colour our reading of their work— something we manage quite easily to avoid when thinking of more distant times.

And yet that doesn't seem a happy or adequate answer; the Thirties were the decade of the Fascism we allow for as well as of the socialism that embarrasses our judgements. I am clearly not yet done with this subject, and will return to it in the next chapter, when I shall have time to say something about the most important and controversial of all these writers, W. H. Auden.

4 · Eros, Builder of Cities

ONE of the chief difficulties of writers compelled by conscience or desire to cross the frontier of class was simply habit, an attachment to their own way of life. An Upward might teach himself to hate that way of life, but even he could not altogether forfeit the inheritance of bourgeois manners and education; and others, though convinced that it must be sacrificed, could not bring themselves to despise it, or to abandon it in what they took to be its last days. The inheritance included certain attitudes very much at variance with the straight-faced and solemn courtship rituals with which they approached the proletariat. They were clever and cliquish, weaned on private jokes and teases which could take a nightmarish turn, as in 'Paid on Both Sides' (1930) and *The Orators* (1933) (both strongly affected by Upward's earlier manner). And they naturally teased one another; and might be expected to comment on what sometimes seemed false or strained in the poses struck in public by friends.

In his posthumous autobiography *The Strings are False* (1965) Louis MacNeice, who was perfectly capable of teasing himself, teased his friends for talking too much about 'barricades' and the like—he might have added 'struggle' and 'history' or even 'love'. There was Stephen Spender, moving forward from liberalism to Communism in a chic apartment with a vulcanite desk and a Wyndham Lewis painting over the fireplace.[1] There was—to focus for a moment on an interesting minor figure in MacNeice's circle —an impassioned Welshman, haranguing a group of writers as if from the pulpit, but not with the object of instructing them in the old ways of virtue; for his message was that in future they must take their orders from the proletariat, lay down their personalities, and become the trumpets of the people, the working class in whom lay all hope of victory in the struggle. The meeting over, the exhausted speaker demanded, and was given, oysters at Prunier's, where oysters were very expensive.

This speaker was Goronwy Rees, not a writer of importance but a

---

[1] This is according to MacNeice. Sir Isaiah Berlin told me after the lecture that there was not a word of truth in it.

figure of some interest to students of bourgeois life and love, and also Oxford, in the Thirties. I say a word about him here because I want at the end of this chapter to distinguish rather sharply between the genuine article and the reproduction, closely associated though they were in the Thirties, as no doubt at other times. MacNeice, who knew him well and liked to take him to rugby internationals at Twickenham, says he would have made 'a wonderful travelling salesman',[2] but he became a Fellow of All Souls instead. Oxford had attached to him that almost irremovable label 'brilliant', and he was famous for charm. By the time I came to know and for a time to work with him the admired black curls were white, but a fair share of folly and misfortune had not quite extinguished the brilliance or the other qualities for which he became well known. I see that there is at present an argument in progress as to whether Rees was ever signed up by the K G B; later it might have been a question rather of the C I A. But it would be a pity if it came to be thought that his association with spies was the only interesting thing about him.

The son of a Welsh preacher, he tells us he had not wanted to go to Oxford, seeing it as the opposite of what he took to be the just order of things; but he soon changed his mind, and congratulated himself on avoiding the corruptions of Cambridge, a university he held responsible not only for the treason of his friends Burgess and MacLean (and doubtless Blunt, about whom Rees remained silent), but for the homosexuality then rampant at Oxford, which he attributed at least in part to the unwise importation from Cambridge of the teachings of G. E. Moore and E. M. Forster. In those days, one gathers, Oxford was a male society, recruited largely from the public schools, and it seems that homosexuality was flaunted as a class marker. The young Welshman found it all very strange, and wondered how it had come about that two universities, one preaching and the other practising corruption, should provide the nation with its rulers as well as with its spies. Nevertheless he quickly joined this decadent society.

However, as the Twenties turned into the Thirties, there was a change of moral climate. For the kind of life Oxford had offered one had now to go to Berlin. Politics, to which nobody had hitherto paid much attention, now became important. In 1931 Rees, already a socialist, became a Prize Fellow of All Souls, with £300 a year, a bed

---

[2] *The Strings are False* (1956), 168.

and board. 'It only slightly marred my enjoyment of it', he writes, 'that an unemployed family in South Wales lived on 30/- a week.' Shortly afterwards he was asked to dinner by Felix Frankfurter, and so met 'the most brilliant undergraduate of his day at Cambridge', Guy Burgess.[3]

Rees justly commends the ruling class of the time for its easy acceptance of a brilliant outsider, even if Welsh, Wesleyan, and heterosexual. And he gives as good an explanation as anybody of how the aestheticism of the Twenties was transformed into the gay Communism of the Thirties. The change was a change of interest rather than of class feeling. And, however easy his acceptance, it is hard to think of Rees as being fully incorporated. Capable of wildness, he was quiet compared with Burgess. He wrote prose of dignified precision, totally lacking in the virtuoso excess of Auden or of his friend Henry Green, famous for his extremely idle and luxurious way of life as an undergraduate. He was loyal to the set he had joined and kept Burgess's secret for sixteen years, revealing it only when Burgess had decamped, but doing so, with ridiculous indiscretion, though that trumpet of the proletariat, the Sunday *People.*

For this performance he got into terrible trouble, and it will doubtless be for his minor role in the Burgess and Blunt affairs, though possibly also for other vagaries, indiscretions, and brilliances, that he will be remembered. But he is also interesting as a charming *métèque,* a talented mimic, a curiosity; very attractive, serious much of the time, unafraid of the *louche* but also of 'big houses where things are done properly'. That phrase comes from Elizabeth Bowen's novel of 1938, *The Death of the Heart,* which is widely and correctly believed to contain a portrait of Rees as a young man. The society represented in the novel has more elegance than conscience: 'The most we can hope for', says one character, 'is to go on getting away with it till the others get it away from us.' 'These days', says another, 'there's something dreadful about talk; people's convictions keep bobbing to the surface, making them flush.' Should one try to earn the respect of the workers (feudalism) or simply pay them for what they do (cash nexus)? In this milieu Eddy seems in a way innocent, like the girl Portia (also a portrait of a well-known and still living writer), who, though a relation, is regarded as of a lower

[3] G. Rees, *A Chapter of Accidents* (1972), 106, 110.

class than the family. However, we are instructed that in such a milieu innocents are forced to be disingenuous: 'the system of our affections is too corrupt for them; so they blunder and cheat and betray.' When Portia runs away it is the perfect servant, Matchett, feudal fossil and ethical norm—her name conventionally reduced to deny her both gender and baptism—who goes after the girl. Matchett's values are not corrupt because she is not involved in that system of affections. Eddy, who partly is, cannot be found at the critical moment, and is therefore, though rather oddly, described by the family as 'a scab'; meanwhile they get on with their dinner.

Eddy is an illustration of Orwell's argument that there can't be lower-class intellectuals because as soon as they become intellectuals they are forced to live in a world very different from their own; and sometimes, we might add, in a system of affections which induces them to blunder and cheat and betray. This was simply an acute form of the problem everybody had when habit or self-interest attached them firmly to a way of life which conscience insisted they should give up; acute because, having but recently arrived at that way of life, one finds it necessary, like some of the other inhabitants, to denounce it in order to be comfortable in it. This could expose one to teasing, as MacNeice, who would never have teased his more important friend Blunt, teased Rees. His revivalist performance at the writers' political gathering was a calculated regression to a nonconformist origin; MacNeice, whose origin was prelatical, couldn't possibly have made such a speech with a straight face. But the lapse was partly redeemed by the amusing request for oysters.

MacNeice wasn't always amused, but he was always conscious of the irony of professing commitment to a cause of which the success would be measured by the degree to which it destroyed the way of life he enjoyed. He was willing to call himself a snob; he liked pleasant places to live, wine, poetry, upper-class women, Greek and Latin classics, in-jokes, and Twickenham better than boiled oranges and Argus-eyed potatoes, and he was reluctant to give them up though sure that they must be given up. Poetry may be sometimes flippant, sometimes sad; but it should always be a civilized admission of this necessity. Minor poet though we may think him, MacNeice —like other poets called minor—did something new, wrote a new poetry of departure, entirely different in tone from the freakish nostalgia of Auden's 'good-bye to the house with its wallpaper red |

Good-bye to the sheets on the warm double bed . . .'.[4] Writing *Autumn Journal* in the aftermath of the fall of Barcelona and the German occupation of Prague, MacNeice feels that more than a sort of comfortable candour is called for, but he is determined not to risk dishonesty. It is because he has the technical resource to be honest that *Autumn Journal* survives as a sensitive record of the failures and successes of a class response to what now seemed a terminal threat. Even in its rehearsal of stock themes I've already mentioned it shows an intelligent blend of sympathy and self-interest.

> August is nearly over, the people
>   Back from holiday are tanned
> With blistered thumbs and a wallet of snaps and a little
>   *Joie de vivre* which is contraband;
> Whose stamina is enough to face the annual
>   Wait for the annual spree,
> Whose memories are stamped with specks of sunshine
>   Like faded *fleurs de lys*.
> Now the till and the typewriter call the fingers,
>   The workman gathers his tools
> For the eight-hour day but, after, the solace
>   Of films or football pools
> Or of the gossip or cuddle, the moments of self-glory
>   Or self-indulgence, blinkers on the eye of doubt,
> The blue smoke rising and the brown lace sinking
>   In the empty glass of stout.

Everything in this passage about duties and pleasures suggests a sympathetic wish that everybody could be as fortunate as the poet, so that one becomes almost too aware of a note of self-congratulation: *our* sprees are more frequent, *our* work less mechanical, *our* consolations more genuine than films and football pools; what *we* do when we cuddle is not called cuddling, and *our* conversation is not just gossip, though we can have that, too. Also we can compare the foam of the Guinness (in *your* glass, not ours, of course) to brown lace. We deplore these contrasts as the result of

> an entirely lost and daft
> System that gives a few at fancy prices
>   Their fancy lives
> While ninety-nine in the hundred who never attend the banquet
>   Must wash the grease of ages off the knives.

[4] *The English Auden*, ed. E. Mendelson (1977), 208–9.

But in spite of this knowledge,

> habit makes me
> Think victory for one implies another's defeat,
> That freedom means the power to order, and that in order
> To preserve the values dear to the élite
> The élite must remain a few. It is so hard to imagine
> A world where the many would have their chance without
> A fall in the intellectual standard of living
> And nothing left that the highbrow cared about.

'Which fears', he continues resolutely, 'must be suppressed.' But the effect of the poem derives from the relaxed way in which it declines to suppress them, though without making too much fuss about the refusal. Neither his personal troubles, delicately alluded to in the poem, nor his purely intellectual complicity with the unwanted revolution, can really prevent this civilized poet from being himself as he waits, somewhat incredulously, for the gun butt to rap on the door.[5] The mind will not follow the heart: 'My sympathies are on the Left. On paper and in the soul. But not in my heart or my guts . . . With my heart and my guts I lament the passing of class.'[6] One could think but not feel the unthinkable.

And that is something we should be able to understand, as we struggle to imagine nuclear winter and carry on as pleasantly as possible with our lives. The war images were different in the Thirties, more thrillingly apocalyptic (Auden's crumbling flood, Empson's forest fire ripening the cones), but they were inevitably based on the recent world conflict, with some imaginative trimmings. At the time of the Spanish Civil War there were great numbers of men around who had fought in France or elsewhere less than twenty years before, and even some who were young enough to fight in the war that was coming: it was expected to be like the Somme, plus aerial bombardment with gas, electric rays, civilian panic.[7] But even after Guernica it smacked for most people of fiction, and the left-wing poets sometimes felt that they were almost alone in their awareness of the historical situation, so that the

---

[5] *Autumn Journal* (1939), 16, 17.
[6] L. MacNeice, *I Crossed the Minch* (1938), 125.
[7] See M. Ceadel, 'Popular Fiction and the Next War', in F. Gloversmith (ed.), *Class Culture and Social Change: A New View of the Thirties* (1980), 161–84.

demands on them were felt as much greater than those to which poets are accustomed, and of a different sort. 'It is quite easy to prove that we are in the first peculiar crisis of civilization,' wrote Geoffrey Grigson, 'and if poets say that rather often now in a good many different ways, is there a fact for us which is more important?'[8] And looking back at those times from a distance of many years, Stephen Spender stressed the isolation of the poets who thought so:

if a small but vociferous and talented minority of what were called 'the intellectuals' (this was the decade in which this term began to be widely used and abused) were almost hypnotically aware of the Nazi nightmare, the vast majority of people—and the government and members of the ruling class—seemed determined to ignore or deny it. One had the sense of belonging to a small group who could see terrible things which no one else saw.[9]

To have that sense was of course to be cut off from the proletariat all over again. The keener one's awareness of imminent war and proletarian revolution, the greater one's difference from the mass of people. It is MacNeice's serious but unimpassioned, rather nostalgic understanding of this that gives *Autumn Journal* some of its value. Others felt they must do something more positive than he—write articles and pamphlets, go to Spain. In the end most came to see that their actions were of small importance, that Spender's 'Who live beneath the shadow of a war, | What can I do that matters?' was the wrong question—a natural, even admirable mistake, rather like the mistake of the Party itself in sending young writers to be killed in Spain. Auden, Day-Lewis, and MacNeice, each in his own way, came to understand this. And, as I said in the previous chapter, Spender, much better informed politically than the others, was forced to conclude that political action in the real world—political action on the only possible side—would be a worse affront to his conscience than abstention. Loyalty to Moscow meant telling lies. It was a simple but decisive consideration.

These were not the first poets to lose faith in a pure revolutionary cause—to become rather desolately aware of the discrepancy between ideals of social justice and the world of political power. Comparisons would, I think, suggest that this group came rather well out of the experience. Such failures are more valuable than some

[8] Quoted in S. Hynes, *The Auden Generation* (1976), 299.
[9] S. Spender, *The Thirties and after* (1978), 33.

successes. Whether or not Auden was right to believe in the end that
poetry can make nothing happen, it must be true that there can be
poetry about the sort of thing that poetry cannot make happen, and
about that failure. Here it might be useful to compare *The Borderers*
and Spender's *Trial of a Judge*, neither work satisfactory to its author
yet central to his development. Wordsworth withheld his play from
publication for almost half a century; Spender has in recent years
given his extensive revision. Of the original version he seems to
accept MacNeice's opinion, that he had intended to express the
weakness of liberalism and the necessity of communism, but that
this intention was 'sabotaged by Spender's unconscious integrity;
the Liberal judge, his example of what-not-to-be, walked away with
one's sympathy'.[10] The play shows that the Judge is wrong when he
says with quiet conviction, 'My truth will win,' and that his enemy
Hummeldorf is equally wrong when he states that 'Abstract justice is
nonsense.' Although the Judge dies in a 'vacuum of misery' he
redeems Hummeldorf; in some sense his truth *has* won, despite the
power of the state to erase or deform the record of its victory. The
play has obvious faults, but it is not a fault that it fails to make the
political point mentioned by MacNeice. At the crisis there is nothing
the Judge can do except suffer, yet the idea of Justice survives him,
whether or not it is to be identified with the hopes of the Communist
prisoners.

In the same year, 1938, Rex Warner published his novel *The
Professor*, a book that deserves to live, not as another tragedy of
liberalism or another indictment of Fascism, but as a study of
abstract justice. The hindsight of the narrator can assure us that the
Professor, summoned to power as his country is about to capitulate
to Fascism, is quite unfitted for politics, believing as he does 'not
only in the existence but in the efficacy of a power more human,
liberal, and kindly than an organization of metal'. Some future
civilization, the narrator allows, may judge the Professor not to have
been entirely without value. However, in his own day he is totally
defeated by the tricks of the Fascists, the follies of non-Communist
labour leaders, and the treachery of a beloved mistress. Possibly his
most important encounter is with a philosophical cobbler, who
wants nothing to do with economic improvement, the amelioration

---

[10]   *The Strings are False*, p. 169.

of poverty, or the cure of disease, holding that infinite human wretchedness is the true ground of love. This rather remarkable passage seems to offer a more abstract version of that love of the poor for their doomed wretchedness so notable in Upward.

In Warner's novel, classrooms, parks, and streets are merely sets before which long serious debates are staged; though sometimes they are invested with a dreamlike terror which reminds one of his earlier book *The Wild Goose Chase* (1937), as well as of Kafka and Upward. These settings seem exactly suited to the impossible logic of the discussions: book-burning, torture, and rape seem to happen in a dream, but when such dreams invade the waking world the existence of justice is signalled only by its absence, and that of love by its present impossibility. This stately, wretchedly noble book, I'm glad to say, is not wholly forgotten. It could not have been written at any other moment, but it still touches the conscience; it expresses very well our interest in justice and our sense of its inaccessibility; and its severity is a reproach to our habit of dismissing books merely because we think their surface ideologies dated.

We do this the more readily when the books in question are so obviously caught up in a slightly embarrassing historical moment, especially when that moment was one of a crisis supremely important in detail and implication to writers conscientiously seeking a direct engagement we know by hindsight to have been unavailable —in the present case, with the immediate issues of poverty, war, and revolution. We know what happened, and cannot re-experience the excitements and terrors of the time, or be assailed in conscience by that set of facts; such reconstructions are impossible even to the most laborious of historians. Instead of smothering ourselves with futile historical fact we rely on convenient mythical formulations to make that past accessible. The myth of the Thirties as a 'low dishonest decade'[11] began to circulate before the decade was over, and, as I said earlier, the influential voice of Orwell helped to give it permanence: its most celebrated writers were a pink clique, a pansy left, enfeebled by a gutless inability to surrender their class privileges. They may have wished to violate frontiers, transgress, defamiliarize the idea of class; but they were too ill-educated and too self-indulgent to do so.

Orwell was a transgressor, a violator of the frontiers of class,

[11] *The English Auden*, p. 245.

including its rhetorical frontier, the one that divided the mandarin from the demotic. One can imagine what he might have said about Rees in Prunier's, and one knows what he said about Auden. Orwell had made many painful enquiries; he knew what it was to be poor, and what it meant to fight and be wounded. These writers who talked a lot but did no first-hand research were not really artists, not really men, not really alive. He thought of them as a transient historical phenomenon. The great writers of the preceding generation hadn't been at public schools or English universities; they had not been Communists; most of them had not even been English. But now the English had swarmed out of their educational reserves and temporarily taken over. The times forbade them to go in for what would have suited them best, 'art for art's sake'. 'Between 1935 and 1939 the Communist Party had an almost irresistible attraction for any writer under forty.' So these young writers joined the Party, or came close to doing so, in much the same way as the previous generation had tended to join the church. They were quite right in their belief that '*laissez-faire* capitalism was finished' but quite wrong to think they must therefore throw in their lot with Stalin. Not to perceive that the Russian Communism then available was nothing more than an instrument of Soviet foreign policy testified to a degree of stupidity possible only to an intellectual or an ignorant working-man. They felt the need of a cause, something to take the place of patriotism, honour, and the like; but they were too ignorant to find a true one. They had no notion of what life was like in countries less fortunate than their own, in police states; for 'cultured' middle-class life in England had 'reached a depth of softness at which a public-school education—five years in a lukewarm bath of snobbery—can actually be looked back on as an eventful period'. Here he is hitting out at Cyril Connolly and his opinion that Eton was an experience after which the rest of life must be something of an anti-climax.

The stick Orwell used to beat these softies in *Inside the Whale* (1940) was, unexpectedly, Henry Miller. Miller wrote strong demotic prose, was, on his own account, heterosexually virile to an unusual degree, and didn't give a damn about the fate of the world. This endeared him to Orwell, who did care about the fate of the world but attached great importance to being demotic and uncommitted. Marxism, he said, could easily prove that 'bourgeois liberty of thought' is an illusion; yet without that illusive liberty 'the creative powers wither away'. Hence the folly of the pink writers in choosing a faith which required its surrender. But it has been part of my argument that these writers were well aware of the difficulty; Upward gives lengthy testimony to the agonies it caused, and the others all came to see that their honest choice was precisely the bourgeois illusion, if illusion it was. Orwell's attack really comes down to saying that they were ignorant, cowardly, and self-regarding, and it is true that they were less tough and less knowing than he was; but they had their own peculiar understanding of their problems and the cost of their solution. They were not quite the half-hearted, the gullible, the gutless Thirties poets of the myth.[12]

The greatest of these poets, Auden, made his own solid contribution to the myth. Arriving in New York on the day Barcelona fell, and failing to go back home when the European war began, he seemed to have declared for bourgeois liberty, however illusive; but that was only the beginning. I agree with Barbara Everett that his move to the United States—hardly the result of a solemn decision—resulted from what he himself diagnosed as a perpetual 'desire for separation', and that it was, at worst, a 'graceless' act.[13] I vaguely remember thinking at the time that he and Isherwood were quite right to make themselves safe, whether or no that was their intention, and I still think this a sensible view of the matter. Anyway, Auden's more substantial contribution to the myth of his own early failure was his wilful and, as I believe, imperceptive renunciation of his own work, his implied denunciation of himself as liar, fraud, or dupe.

Despite some quite strongly expressed views to the contrary, Auden remains at the centre of our thinking about the Thirties, and it will not seem inappropriate if I conclude this chapter by discussing him at slightly greater length than I have so far. I will begin by mentioning one of the more celebrated instances of his meddlings and recantations, the 'Prologue' to *Look, Stranger!* (a title I may be alone in preferring to Auden's own choice, *On This Island*, for it sets him at a distance from this island, affords those panoramic views of what he did not know and meant to find out). I have for fifty years thought the 'Prologue' a great poem and I don't suppose anything could induce me to change my view at this stage, though I admit that believing it to be so may have affected my notion of what one sort of

[12] G. Orwell, *Selected Essays* (Penguin edn. 1957), 9-50.
[13] B. Everett, *Poets in their Time* (1986), 220.

great poem should be like. But Auden himself was very unhappy with it, messed it about, and later dropped it altogether from his canon.

Edward Mendelson, who probably knows more about Auden than anybody else does, and certainly a lot more than I do, has always championed the poet's decisions in such cases, and he does so here, calling the 'Prologue', along with some other poems, 'deeply self-contradictory or inauthentic'. He points to May 1932, the month in which the poem was written, as the moment of a major change in Auden's manner, a switch 'from clinical distance to didactic exhortation'. His admiration of the final lines of the poem is muted; here they are:

> In bar, in netted chicken-farm, in lighthouse,
> Standing on these impoverished constricting acres,
> The ladies and gentlemen apart, too much alone,
>
> Consider the years of the measured world begun,
> The barren spiritual marriage of stone and water.
> Yet, O, at this very moment of our hopeless sigh
>
> When inland they are thinking their thoughts but are watching these
> islands.
> As children in Chester look to Moel Fammau to decide
> On picnics by the clearness or withdrawal of her treeless crown,
>
> Some possible dream, long coiled in the ammonite's slumber,
> In uncurling, prepared to lay on our talk and kindness
> Its military silence, its surgeon's idea of pain;
>
> And out of the Future into actual History,
> As when Merlin, tamer of horses, and his lords to whom
> Stonehenge was still a thought, the Pillars past
>
> And into the undared ocean swung north their prow,
> Drives through the night and star-concealing dawn
> For the virgin roadsteads of our hearts an unwavering keel.[14]

'Splendid as this rhetoric is', says Mendelson, '—and the retention of the subject of the verb *drives* until the end is splendid indeed—it leaves some doubts . . .' For instance, 'Merlin, tamer of horses' is inappropriate, since, if Merlin follows Dante's Ulysses beyond the Pillars of Hercules, his fate should be that of Ulysses, not millennium but disaster. Mendelson catalogues faults and loosenesses elsewhere in the poem, and Auden's thefts from Anthony Collett's book *The*

---

[14] *The English Auden*, p. 119.

Changing Face of England (1926, cheap edition May 1932, the very month of the poem) are, it is implied, further evidence of opportunism and inauthenticity.[15]

It is likely enough that Auden himself would have accepted these criticisms, but they seem misplaced all the same. The poem isn't truly didactic, for it doesn't teach—it prophesies, with a reminiscence of John of Gaunt. In the Newton passage condemned by Mendelson, Love (that now vast impersonal force, the Eros that builds cities and reforms societies) is addressed like this:

Here too on our little reef display your power,
This fortress perched on the edge of the Atlantic scarp,
The mole between all Europe and the exile-crowded sea;

And make us as Newton was, who in his garden watching
The apple falling towards England, became aware
Between himself and her of an eternal tie.

This is surely a very just conceit. England is little, a reef, a fortress, a mole; it is seen, like everything else in the poem, from a height, a distance; on one side Europe threatens, on the other the sea (enriched by the epithet 'exile-crowded', which makes it a nowhere full of anxious transients, in contrast to our home, our known and loved bit of territory, the garden in which, if anywhere, we walk in peace). It is to this small spot, a rock sticking out of the ocean, that gravity impelled the apple of Newton, thus demonstrating that the power which maintains the constellations is a perfect figure for the way we perceive, in our tiny habitat, the operation of another cosmic force, here called Love, which also moves the sun and the other stars.

As for the debt to Collett, it was noticed long ago in a review of *Look, Stranger!* by Janet Adam Smith, who attributed it, admiringly, to Auden's sensible habit of hoarding phrases.[16] Collett's book is already a hoard of phrases, and, given the sort of book it is, a poet of Auden's cast, with a passion for panoramic views and long historical perspectives, would have been mad not to use it. Its very title – *The Changing Face of England*—is exact for the period; but to see how apt the book was we need to observe that the changes Collett talks about are large-scale—geological, ethological, philological, and this is what enabled Auden to project his sense of catastrophic political change on

[15] E. Mendelson, *Early Auden* (1982), 246, 142.
[16] Reprinted in J. Haffenden (ed.), *W. H. Auden: The Critical Heritage* (1983), 231.

to the scale of those vast but slower upheavals that change our coast, our rivers, and our language. It is a magnificent book, now of course out of date; changes Collett describes as occurring have now occurred, and his patriotic musings on race would certainly be called racist. But he has real grandeur and real point. What, to mention the most famous borrowing, what could better illustrate the relation of England to the continent as one of unity in separation than the remark Auden brilliantly stole for the great chorus in *The Dog beneath the Skin*?[17] There Collett's observation that the North Sea 'is still so shallow that if St Paul's was planted anywhere between the Dutch and English coasts the golden cross would shine above the water' is repeated with no more modification than Shakespeare would make to suitable bits of Plutarch. And Collett, in this modern version of the *Mutability Cantos*, dwells on the instability of what may seem fixed boundaries, the land liquefied by the sea, the sea as it were solidified by the land, the apparently eternal boundaries always in flux. A poet who likes to look on this island like the hawk or the helmeted airman could hardly do better than use Collett as a chart, showing the immemorial cliffs that are yet so new in geological time that solidity cannot be expected of them—'Like the moulting crab they need time before their surface hardens'—and then closing in on the curled ammonites as the poet had done on the cigarette-end smouldering in a garden border. Auden, remembered the ammonites, was grateful to learn about the Sugarloaf standing sentinel over Abergavenny and the children in Chester scanning the summit of Moel Fammau to judge the weather prospects. Years later he must have thought of Collett when he wrote 'In Praise of Limestone'; and perhaps when he used the Welsh word 'nant' to mean a brook·or burn. Collett's book offered him language that was already on the way to being poetry, a view and a love of England close to his own, the cosmic force intensely felt in one's own garden yet known as universal; and a certainty that change is the law of the world.

   That is why Merlin (a Trojan, therefore a proto-Briton) turns *north* from the Pillars, not south like Dante's Ulysses (a Greek) and finds not destruction but England, when England was not yet even a thought. The ancient possible dream will arrive in the same way to transform the impoverished constricting acres. Auden quite enjoys telling us it won't be comfortable, that it's no use raising a shout, that

17   *The English Auden*, p. 281.

our talk and kindness will have to be laid away because they existed only for 'ten persons'. It was for this kind of talk—'its military silence, its surgeon's idea of pain'—that some admired him and some, like Orwell, thought him too ready to speak of what he didn't understand. But now, I think, we can see that it has its own accuracy. This is how it feels to contemplate a future, long prefigured by history, and now imminent, over which you have no control and from which you can expect no comfort save that of conscience and compliance. It will be a catastrophe, but of the sort Auden would later have called a eucatastrophe.

So that last sentence of the poem isn't to be dismissed as mere rhetoric, however splendid. It celebrates, with the aid of its extended simile and the mythic charge it carries, an improbable, even a painful victory for goodness, for history as impersonal and alarming but ultimately benign—a victory as epoch-making as the one Auden celebrated almost thirty years later in the poem 'Hammerfest', when he spoke eucatastrophically of

> . . . that preglacial Actium when the huge
> Archaic shrubs went down before the scented flowers,
> And earth was won for color . . .[18]

But that palaeobotanical victory happened, and the voyages of the Trojan Merlin and the possible dream didn't, so that, when Auden decided that 'nothing is lovely, | Not even poetry, which is not the case',[19] he concluded that such poems as the 'Prologue' were mendacious as well as useless. Certainly the 'Prologue' did not reduce the crowd of exiles, hasten the millennium, or even, in all probability, win recruits for the Party. Its usefulness, if it has any, is as a prophecy of love and its attendant terror.

Something of the sort may be said also of *Spain, 1937*. We all remember Orwell's sneer at 'the conscious acceptance of guilt in the necessary murder'—'it could only have been written by a person to whom murder is at most a *word*'—but fewer recall that he also described the poem as 'one of the few decent things that have been written about the Spanish war'. Stephen Spender, who thinks it a rare attempt on Auden's part to write a poem with the formal structure of the dialectic, feels that it expresses 'an attitude which for a few weeks or months he felt intellectually forced to adopt, but

---

[18] *Collected Poems* (1976), 546.   [19] Ibid. 433.

which he never truly felt'.[20] Mendelson accepts the poet's own judgement, which is that, like 'September 1, 1939', it is 'infected with incurable dishonesty'—a dishonesty which, according to Mendelson, lies in its 'implicit claim to have joined the realm of the private will to that of the public good, when in fact the union had been made through the force of rhetoric alone'. This distrust of 'rhetoric'—after all the only instrument available for the purpose —the critic has inherited from the poet, and he gives the word a very restricted sense, associating it, I suppose, with propaganda. However, he allows that neither *Spain* nor 'September 1, 1939' is simply 'public and didactic', calling them 'equivocal',[21] as indeed they are. Sometimes I find it hard to believe that Auden could have so badly misunderstood his own poems unless it was from a simple desire to escape the memory of what it had been like to write them. Anyway, I believe that both Spender and Mendelson, despite their closeness to the poet and his work, are wrong about *Spain*.

In 1937 the Spanish Civil War seemed to have simplified the great historical issues by offering a plain though painful choice; as Spender expressed it, an individual could believe that his own action or failure to act 'could lead to the winning or losing of [that war], could even decide whether or not the Second World War was going to take place'.[22] The government seemed not to care much, even when British ships were bombed, and it might have seemed that the masses went on with their 'dreams of freedom'[23] and did not bother about the other dream uncurling from the ammonite, the tidal wave that would soon breach 'the dykes of our content'[24]—the satisfactions of the middle class, or of the poor content with the pools, the odd cuddle, the bitter beer, and the annual baring of flesh 'beside the undiscriminating sea'.[25] If Auden came to think it wrong or hopeless to write poems intended to move some parts of that large public, it is not difficult to understand why he went on to join the party of his detractors and deplore his own past.

But *Spain* is not a marching song or a recruiting poster; it is an attempt to express what it feels like to confront a great historical crisis. At bottom such crises have elements in common, and in this respect Auden's poem resembles Marvell's 'Horatian Ode'—indeed in my view it is our best political poem except for Marvell's. Both

---

[20] *The Thirties and after*, p. 30.
[22] *The Thirties and after*, p. 25.
[24] Ibid. 138.

[21] *Early Auden*, pp. 200–3.
[23] *The English Auden*, p. 155.
[25] Ibid. 138.

deal with the great work of time and its ruin, with individual will and its relation to historical forces. Both have wit and magniloquence, and both are, in Mendelson's word, 'equivocal'. As the execution of Charles (which divides Marvell's poem in half) divides one age from another—however much one might regret the past and hesitate before the unknown future—so Spain divides history and concentrates attention on today and its 'struggle'. 'Tomorrow, *perhaps*, the future . . .' The skewed detail, its oddity and force, may strike us as too much of their period, but the strong build of the poem supports them, as Marvell's supports his puns and conceits.

Auden came to hate the last stanza most of all:

> The stars are dead; the animals will not look:
> We are left alone with our day, and the time is short and
>   History to the defeated
> May say Alas but cannot help or pardon—[26]

and yet it seems to me exactly right. Heaven and earth leave us to our moment; choice is necessary, failure irredeemable. When he said this was 'unforgiveable', Auden had changed his mind about history and redemption; but that cannot hurt the poem, which ends with a remark as clear-sighted and as urgent as that which ends Marvell's poem: 'The same arts that did gain | A power, must it maintain;' 'History to the defeated | May say Alas but cannot help or pardon.' The ideas are ancient, the politics modern; and so too with the individual poetic response.

So *Spain* does deal with what is the case, even if the poet came to see it as a reflection of an uneasy or shaming interlude in his intellectual life. There is the past, wittily sketched as a history of instruments —the counting-frame, the cathedral, the dynamo—and a future less clearly definable; there is Life, an evolutionary force that once operated independently, as when it established 'the robin's plucky canton', but whose action now depends on human decision. Life is now boldly identified with Spain, which at this critical moment offers itself to human choice. Henceforth the forces of life, like Marvell's 'ancient rights', will 'hold or break | As men are strong or weak'. They tell you to choose, not what to choose. The whole of history, evolutionary as well as cultural, culminates at this moment, and in Spain—a figure for crisis and necessary choice, a reef or mole between past and future. We have always projected our individual

---

[26] *The English Auden* p. 212.

crises on to history, so Spain is caught up in a typology, and it is the nature of typologies to transcend history; because we all at times have to make more or less desperate choices, the urgency of that Spanish moment does not disappear with the moment itself. It becomes part of our mythical habit. It is this validity of type, as well as its magniloquence and wit, that preserves Auden's poem.

My brief doesn't require me to argue that Auden was never glib or false; as he said later, he was always a British Pharisee,[27] not as other men were, and lacking the sense other men might have that they needed at least to seem consistent in their opinions, or to give plausible reasons for changing them. Auden, I think, never really bothered to do that, and there is good reason not to accept his Thirties poetry at his own valuation. It was written under conditions of considerable intellectual discomfort, at a time when, in Spender's phrase, there was a real compulsion 'to make some choice outside the entanglements of our private life'.[28] The effort to do that enabled Auden to discover an appropriate magniloquence, something that was to recur very rarely in his work over the following thirty years, because he falsely equated it with falsity.

Auden once said of Kipling that poem after poem of his deals with encirclement, danger, and fear, 'vague menacing shapes which can be kept away by incessant action but can never be finally overcome'.[29] There is something of Auden himself in this description. He feared encirclement—Spain and Thirties politics, each in its way, were something of the kind; they invaded the mind from all points of the compass; and, lacking Kipling's ability to build bulwarks, Auden simply—or not so simply—withdrew. There was poetry in the being afraid of encirclement and in the departure from the ring as well; in the attempt to be on the side of Eros, builder of cities, as well as in the abandonment of Eros in favour of Agape.

I began this chapter with some words on a minor figure, Goronwy Rees, who was part of the network of acquaintance that included both the poets and the spies who trafficked more or less lovingly between upper-class life and the politics of proletarian revolution; and I have ended it by discussing a major poet who belonged to the same connection. I did so because I hoped the differences between the two might be instructive. The terms of abuse and the terms of the

---

[27] *Collected Poems*, p. 581.   [28] *The Destructive Element* (1935), 223.
[29] *Forewords and Afterwords*, ed. E. Mendelson (1973).

myth can hardly fit both cases. When Auden talks about 'the struggle' he is engaged in one, and writing a poetry which, with all its virtuosity, is a poetry of struggle. This is not done by bullying other writers into accepting the virtue, beauty, and power of the proletariat. If we can't tell the difference between these responses it may be that we no longer understand the peculiar stimuli which produced them, both the honourable and the not so honourable. They were apocalyptic, or at least sham apocalyptic, and, as I remarked earlier, our apocalyptic sympathies are probably exhausted now that apocalypse, which used to be a moment, has become an epoch, not a threat of Armageddon so much as a permanent migraine. The modern Irish poets know something about struggle, and the entanglements of private and public life, but we are dulled. On the léft, it seems to me, thinking grows more and more rarefied and academic, less and less intimate, or desirous of intimacy, with the life of the people, with the threat of encirclement, with crisis as a condition more than merely notional. It takes an Upward, a lonely old warrior never not to be committed, never not aware of the need for action, to speak now of CND as then, long ago, he spoke of the Party, as a shield against the last destructive assaults of a dying capitalism.

I don't of course mean that one has to join some group or party in order to apprehend what is valuable in Thirties bourgeois literature, and to allow for the distortions caused by historical myths of convenience. The effort required is critical and historical; if we make it we may come to honour what is too often calumniated without much examination—a literature that is often splendid in the moment of its enforced engagement with the almost unthinkable Other —across the frontier, almost cut off, encircled, but capable of fineness even in its moment of withdrawal.

What I have been trying to tell is, in its way, a love-story, almost a story of forbidden love. If asked to define that huge word I will not repeat my reference to the Eros of Freud, or to Caudwell's amorous economics, but simply repeat a definition of love Auden himself once gave: 'intensity of attention.'[30] He might well have been thinking of the uneasy passion with which he looked at 'the defeated and disfigured',[31] or at Spain, or at his friends' encircled lives.

[30] W. H. Auden, review of V. Clifton, *The Book of Talbot*, in *The English Auden*, p. 319.   [31] *The English Auden*, p. 156.

PART TWO

History and Value

5 · Value at a Distance

Dr Johnson began his Preface to Shakespeare with what is, I suppose, the best-known treatment of the topic of the continuance of literary fame. He admits that there are people who reverence the old 'not from reason, but from prejudice. Some seem to admire indiscriminately whatever has been long preserved, without considering that time has sometimes co-operated with chance.' But he is nevertheless sure that to what we should call works of the imagination 'no other test can be applied than length of duration and continuance of esteem'. Johnson doesn't make much of his point, that chance may have a part in their continuance, nor does he say in whose esteem they must endure. And, although we are living in a period when academic literary critics are peculiarly apt to ask questions about what it is that they suppose themselves to be doing, the issue of value comes up mostly in the course of factional challenges to the institutional consensus, when the arguments tend to be about political power rather than about the value of particular books. Questions about the value past literature may be thought to have in itself, if asked, tend to get dogmatic and ineffectual answers. We are happy to relinquish the whole question to that useful allegorical figure, Time. Time, we say, will separate the sheep from the goats. But, as Heywood Broun wisely remarked, posterity—or Time—is just as likely to be wrong as anybody else.[1] It is people who sort them out, by neglecting them, accepting them because they are told to, expounding them in ways that ensure that others will or won't read them.

Among the problems to be met in any attempt to comment on this state of affairs the hardest is probably that of historical distance—the inevitable loss of immediate historical context. This can, indeed must, obscure the original sense of a text. The original balance between novelty and familiarity is bound to be lost, and the discrepancy between the sense it originally had and the sense we find in it has an obvious bearing on the whole question of value. If we have lost most or all sense of whatever value the original offered, what is it

---

[1] In *The Oxford Book of Aphorisms*, ed. J. Gross (1983), 322.

that we now find valuable? Some people are confident that there is an immanent value which, in spite of the continuous changes forced upon interpreters so long as the work is read, remains, and probably remains in some sense constant in different temporal contexts. This is the value that enables the work to pass the test of time. Such, more or less, is the position of Anthony Savile in a book which bears the title *The Test of Time* (1982). Savile pays no attention to the kind of thing Gadamer might say about his view, but he does take on Adorno and the belief, acceptance of which would be awkward for his own thesis, that great art, especially in the past century or so, must be in conflict with contemporary ideologies. For he happens to think that 'what a work of art expresses it expresses by reliance on a correspondence that the artist and his audience find peculiarly natural between expressive form and what it is that form is found expressive of' (p. 295). So we shall best understand survival by consulting 'the best available contemporary reading' (p. 68). (How we are to decide on the best is a question.) This reading will afford a canonical interpretation which, nurtured by tradition, will guarantee a pass in the test of time, at any rate if the examiners are drawn from that 'core of persons who give the culture its character' (p. 11). It is for them to perpetuate the best contemporary reading, and so justify the unchanging value of the work.

To many this position must seem wrong. For one thing it ignores the discrepancy of which I spoke, the discrepancy between an original sense and any sense that can now be found. Every kind of hermeneutics has to deal with this discrepancy, but because it is of central importance to Marxists I shall, in this chapter, say a little about the ways in which they have dealt with it.

The issue had particular urgency in the Thirties, when it seemed essential to decide on the value of existing bourgeois art in the age of the revolutionary proletariat—an age, it was hoped, that would produce its own very different kind of art. Behind that immediate and particular problem there lay a more general one that still bothers us. Can literature participate directly in social or political action if it is truly literature? Isn't literature that is truly literature silently defined as writing which can't do so?

Let me consider the historically limited version of the problem by saying something about a novel that aspired to be a work of that new type—literature that was yet meant to have a direct practical effect. This book is now forgotten, I think, by that core of persons who give the culture its character, though remembered by a political minority which would like to make drastic changes in more orthodox canonical systems in order to rehabilitate just such works, of which the Thirties saw a good many. Members of this minority believe that, if they in their turn could become that core of persons, there would be drastic changes in what passed for valuable literature.

Lewis Jones, born in 1897, was a miner in the Rhondda. He was politically active from an early age, and in 1923 he won a scholarship to the Central Labour College in London. During his time there he joined the Communist Party. In 1926 he served a three-month prison sentence for seditious speeches, and after the failure of the General Strike led the last-ditch resistance of the Welsh miners to non-union labour. He organized hunger marches and demonstrations against the Means Test, and in 1936 campaigned ardently for the Popular Front. In January 1939, on the evening of a day in which he had spoken to thirty audiences on behalf of Spanish Aid, he suddenly died, at the age of forty-one. He had achieved much celebrity as an orator, but had also written two novels, *Cwmardy* published in 1937, and a sequel, *We Live*, which appeared after his death, in 1939.[2]

Jones, then, was a committed political activist, and he was not writing novels in a spirit of disinterest. He has lately won the attention of some young left-wing critics in search of a genuine proletarian novel—that is, a working-class novel which succeeds in converting to socialist purposes a realism with deep historical roots in a bourgeois genre. There must be no trace of 'bourgeois individualism'; the hero will be a class, a collectivity. *Cwmardy*, though it focuses on a small group of characters, offers a documentary history of the coalfield and its people from the last years of the nineteenth century up to 1921. *We Live* continues the story to the time of writing. Jones explains that the books were written 'during odd moments stolen from mass meetings, committees, demonstrations, marches, and other activities', and says they are the work *of* a collectivity as well as works *about* a collectivity.

The central character, based on the author himself, is deprived of his job and sent to prison because of his militancy. The older generation of miners is represented by his boisterous father, a man of prodigious strength which is rapidly wearing out as he moves into

---

[2] See the Introductions of David Smith to the Lawrence and Wishart reprints of 1978.

his sixties. Family feeling is strong, and the hero has a happy marriage, but larger political conflicts are reflected in life at home; the wife's father is an old-style Labour leader, once respected and successful, later forced to compromise with the bosses and accused of betraying the workers. Yet membership of the Party still has something shameful about it, at any rate in the eyes of respectable Labour and chapel people, as well as those of the mineowners and the police.

The detail of conflict is intimate and interesting—the tactics of the owners and the responses of the workers, caught between a union that seems too ready to compromise and a Party operating from distant London. The owners' case for wage reductions, increased work loads, and so forth, is not understated. Lord Cwmardy is a sentimental old fellow with a real affection for the miners and especially for their singing; but his financial problems override his sympathies. Protest is met by lock-out, the deliberate separating of friends in the pits, and the importation of cheap labour from elsewhere. The police turn brutal, often provoking riots for which men go to prison.

The workers are given the best arguments, of course, but the notation of poverty, injury, fatigue, and illness is on the whole unsentimental, and the account of the plight of the miners' families after the failure of the General Strike, when they were left to carry on alone and without strike pay, is extremely persuasive. There are some remarkable crowd scenes. Jones, like other proletarian novelists, needs to be especially on his mettle at such moments, for here if anywhere he can reconcile a propagandist purpose with the virtues of a realism invented by a class enemy; at such points 'good writing' and Communist realism have to cohabit. This is where the collectivity gets on to the page; the hills round Cwmardy are black with marching men and women, banners flying and bands competing with one another. And the hero is simply absorbed into the mass:

Len momentarily felt himself like a weak straw drifting in and out with the surge of bodies. Then something powerful swept through his being as the mass soaked its strength into him, and he realised that the strength of them all was the measure of his own, that his existence and power as an individual was buried in that of the mass now pregnant with motion behind him. The momentous thought made him inhale deeply and his chest expanded, throwing his head erect and his shoulders square to the breeze that blew the banners into red rippling slogans of defiance and action . . .'[3]

[3] *We Live* (1939; 1978 edn.), 243.

The climax is a stay-down strike. The blackness of the pit, the makeshift domestic arrangements, the feeding of the horses, and so on, are very well done, and the success of the strike is recorded with much exuberance. However, the novel doesn't end with this local victory but with the war in Spain, and Len's heroic death—easily identified as sentimental propaganda, and so offering a good target to enemies of proletarian fiction.

Carole Snee, a Marxist champion of these books, believes they do exactly what proletarian novels ought to do: they exile bourgeois individualism and present a class as the central character. Private problems are always reflections of the political struggle. But to speak of Jones as having successfully introduced 'a proletarian consciousness' into fiction seems a bit excessive.[4] What most betrays the lingering bourgeois taint, if that is what we want to call it, is a tendency to posh overwriting. There is a good deal of this kind of thing:

The wind howled over the mountains and swept down on Cwmardy as though chased by a million nightmares. . . . Street lamps turned the moisture into miniature rainbows that glistened on the slimy road . . . the pit spewed two trams full of coal into the storm and sucked two empties out of it. The wind howled more loudly still at the theft, but to no avail. . . . The heavy wooden droppers on the shaft-head beat back the chasing wind and rain, which sought revenge on the houses lower down the valley.[5]

Such writing damages the proletarian image, clogs the message with fancy creative-writing-course prose, and it is clearly written under the impression that this is how good writers write; Orwell would have seen in it an illustration of what he took to be an inevitable process, the kidnapping of working-class writers by the bourgeoisie the minute they put pen to paper. The only way to write plainly, as a worker should, would be to write like Orwell. But the plain style is a middle-class accomplishment, got by arduous and educated rhetorical efforts. In Jones's posher bits of prose, and his occasional glamorization of the workers, working-class pastoral takes over from proletarian realism; heroic, loving, loyal, and tragic gestures

---

[4] 'Working-class Literature or Proletarian Writing?', J. Clark. M. Heinemann, D. Margolies, and C. Snee (eds.), *Culture and Crisis in Britain in the Thirties* (1979), 165–91.
[5] *We Live*, p. 1.

are recorded and admired as if from the outside; fine writing takes place.

Yet there is plenty of indication elsewhere that Jones, in spite of his job as a Party organizer and his aspirations as a writer, remained close to the community he was talking about. He conveys much more than any outsider could about strike diet, accidental death, routine police brutality, grubbing for coal on tips, or simply the way people sit in their kitchens and talk. And who, on the outside, is qualified to say whether his association of Communism with the joys of marital love is mere sentimentality? It was a fantasy shared by some bourgeois writers of the time, the notion that the emotions and mutual dependencies of a man and his wife could somehow be extended on to a vast collective scale. Jones's husband and wife address each other as 'Comrade' even at moments of tenderness. But we find this and other things a little odd, a little embarrassing, and this inclines us to say that the book is very much of its moment, a very short moment indeed; and that Jones could not avoid what seems to be a falsity inherent in the form; and that his work is at best worth a place in the archive as a document in the history of taste or social fashion.

I doubt if Jones was much admired in his own day by the very bourgeois intellectuals who wanted so desperately to discover a genuine proletarian writing which would reconcile art and Communism, yet still made inherited assumptions about the nature of art. How could this blend of bourgeois fiction and naked propaganda be 'good writing'? We should have less difficulty fifty years on; after all, we are continually dealing with other kinds of literature that reflect dead or distasteful ideologies and we do not feel bound to allow those dead ideologies to determine literary value. Perhaps if we could be induced to extend to Jones the favours we do Yeats, ranting about eugenics, or Pound, ranting about Jewish finance, we might take a different view of his achievement. But it seems we can't. Why?

Let us look for a moment at a contemporary piece of writing about mines and miners upon which it is still customary to place a high value. This is Orwell's chapter called 'Down the Mine', from *The Road to Wigan Pier* (1937). Orwell is here using all his skill to offer what seems to be a sober documentary of life below ground, whereas Jones is more the equivalent of a Russian propaganda film of the period. I agree that Orwell's chapter is finely written. Yet down the mine with Jones you feel an ease, a familiarity with the machines and tools, with the conversation and physical condition of the workers, and the simple economics of their obligation to fill quotas, that Orwell does not even pretend to have. His work is offered as the sedentary writer's equivalent of the collier's; it has a deliberately sustained workmanlike quality, the artist is at his coalface. At the same time he emphasizes how impossible it would be for him, or any sedentary person, to do *their* work, or even get to *their* coalface without exhaustion. There is the pastoral note of envy—with an overtone of that sexual interest in the completely other that one often sees in the bourgeois writing of the period—when he speaks of the physical beauty of the miners, of their 'most noble bodies; wide shoulders tapering to slender supple waists, and small pronounced buttocks and sinewy thighs, with not an ounce of waste flesh anywhere. . . . driving their huge shovels under the coal with stupendous force and speed'.[6]

In Jones's book the son of the coalowner goes down the pit on a conciliatory visit to the stay-down strikers. He is a twenty-year-old undergraduate. Len receives him roughly, pointing to a pitboy of fourteen as a source of the money that keeps the young man idle at twenty. To the miners this youth with his 'magnificent body' stands for what they cannot have; he is taller, healthier than men who are enfeebled by their abnormal labour and the coaldust they continually breathe.[7] For them there is health above, fatigue and sickness below ground. It is Orwell who sees the miners as images of power and beauty, cut off from the sicklier world above by 'hundreds of yards of solid rock, bones of extinct beasts, subsoil, flints, roots of growing things, green grass and cows grazing on it'. Jones's miners feel above them only the weight of class oppression. Orwell emphasizes the general importance of the miners' labour—without it, he says, there could be no novels, no bread, no war, and no revolution; theirs is work 'so vitally necessary and yet so remote from our experience, so invisible, as it were, that we are capable of forgetting it as we forget the blood in our veins', though without it superior

[6] *The Road to Wigan Pier* (1937; 1965 edn.), 25. It is fair to say that Orwell does give minute details of miners' wages, hygiene, and eating habits, though always, quite naturally, from the viewpoint of a sympathetic observer rather than a participant. And I should add that *The Road to Wigan Pier* is the best possible introduction to the general topic of bourgeois intellectual attitudes to the condition of England in the Thirties.

[7] *We Live*, pp. 110–11.

persons could not remain superior. But to Jones's miners their work *is* the blood in their veins, and it is expended to make others rich. In good writing on this subject, it seems, the *others* must be the miners.

Orwell's is the reaction of an involuntarily superior person, recognizing with amazement and some humility an otherness, an exploited strength, that is certainly relevant to an account of the divisions imposed by capitalism, but which, because of the nature of that recognition—the gleaming iron bodies, the infernal character of the mine—virtually breaks free from such political considerations. In the diary he kept while preparing his book, Orwell records facts about pay, housing, and diet—rather superior Mass Observation material, excluded from the finished piece. He also says there that he suspected working-class Communists. Never for a moment did he see himself as anything but an investigator come in from another world.[8] His way of knowing the world of the miners derives from the other world; and this despite his extraordinary efforts to familiarize himself with theirs. It was from his world, not theirs, that writers came.

The problem is not peculiar to the Thirties, though it presented itself then with a peculiar sharpness. There were different ways of handling it—Edward Upward, for instance, was well aware that his Communist faith originated in his class, that as a writer what he wanted was to retreat into some comfortable privacy and write, though the times seemed to require him to do otherwise—'to hunger, work illegally, and be anonymous'—to get rid of bourgeois preferences, love a whole alien class, and write, with immense difficulty, a book that could show his talent to be reconcilable with his commitment.

Few of us would even bother to compare Jones's achievements with those of Orwell or Upward; yet, although his faith is the same as Upward's, he is still what Upward could only strive to be, a proletarian, taking his megaphone into the proletarian streets and loving the miners not because they were strange or beautiful but out of long habit, convinced that the sort of society they had made might be transfigured yet remain something quite other than a bourgeois good society, convinced that his writing could help to bring this about.

[8] *Collected Essays, Journalism and Letters*, ed. S. Orwell and I. Angus (1968), i. 170–214.

But the lack in his work is one he couldn't possibly remedy, or want to—a writer's sense of the remoteness, the otherness, of the workers, and especially of miners; that otherness which is not merely an otherness of class, but of aesthetic presumptions. Even Lawrence, who was born among them, developed a mystique about miners, their 'latent wildness and unbrokenness', their darker life, their blood knowledge, gaiety, love of whippets, drink, dancing, and sex. No doubt there is truth in this idea of them; but the otherness is more important than the verisimilitude. That is why Orwell left much everyday detail of life above ground in his notebook. In art, the core of cultured persons will if only from habit prefer the more distant, mythical, pastoral view to the factuality of the proletarian novel, as written by insiders. It is not the overtness of Jones's politics that determines his failure so much as his exclusion from acceptable—that is, bourgeois—modes of rendering the proletariat as other. That his attempts were made in the form of the novel, the great bourgeois invention, and that they occasionally contain pseudo-bourgeois fine writing, only makes their failure more conspicuous.

There were some heroic attempts to reconcile art with political engagement. But perhaps they couldn't be reconciled. Assumptions about art and value were simply too deeply rooted; and they were often shared by the very people who most wanted a proletarian art. And so the whole question of the relation of a revolutionary pro-letariat to bourgeois art became acute. It was not only a test of the bourgeois political conscience; it raised the apparently very urgent question as to how the whole heritage of past art would be treated in a Communist state. This was a difficult issue, calling for the applica-tion to an immediate political problem of abstract considerations in aesthetics and the philosophy of history.

Even as a matter of day-to-day political action there had to be decisions about writing. Should bourgeois writers sympathetic to the cause be allowed to write for the cause, or, in the United States, to join the John Reed clubs, which sought a new proletarian art completely severed from the art of the past? Would their skills, tainted as they were, serve the cause as well as a purer though less skilful working-class commitment? In such circumstances the Americans tended to be more explicit than the English about both doctrine and its consequences. Here is Louis Kronenberger in 1937:

There is really no fundamental dilemma. It is more necessary for us to interest ourselves in an important subject treated without much merit than in an unimportant subject treated with considerable merit. *Culture herself* demands that we put the right social values ahead of the right literary values, and whenever we encounter people who want to keep art dustproof, who bewail the collapse of 'aesthetic values', it is our duty to ascertain just how far their indignation is a screen for reactionary and unsocial thing.

Kronenberger adds that 'cultural coarsening' is inevitable in a period of stress, and the present business of writers is to save civilization rather than enrich it. Truth is important; but cutting out 'the cancers of society' is more important. Culture is a cathedral in which at the moment we have no time to pray; the best we can hope to do is to protect it from bombardment.

Here you can see the cultural dilemma. How sharply Kronenberger, a revolutionary for the nonce, distinguishes between revolutionary imperatives and artistic 'merit'! How absolute his antithesis between 'aesthetic values' and social justice! His was the plight of many bourgeois writers flung into a situation where skills derived from an oppressive culture were to be put at the disposal of the dispossessed—in which 'bad' writing on the important subject was more important than 'good' writing on non-revolutionary subjects. Quoting Kronenberger's article in his essay on Communist criticism, Edmund Wilson commends its honesty but wonders what it means in practice—telling lies about Trotsky? Praising boring novels about textile strikes and condemning Wilder or Hemingway?[9] The rhetorical question makes clear Wilson's assumption that 'good' writing doesn't make direct political interventions.

But there were some who would have dismissed Wilson as a traitor and even Kronenberger as a trimmer. They thought the new order required the overthrow of all previous notions about literary value. At the 1934 conference of the British Section of the International Union of Revolutionary Writers Alec Brown declared that 'literary English from Caxton to us is an artificial jargon of the ruling class'. He was advocating a breach with that tradition more total than any that ever gained the approval of the Russian Communist Party.[10]

---

[9] *The Shores of Light* (1937; 1952 edn.), 647–9.
[10] Quoted by H. Gustav Klaus, 'Socialist Fiction in the 1930s: Some Preliminary Observations', in J. Lucas (ed.), *The Thirties: A Challenge to Orthodoxy* (1978), 13–41.

That the Communist or pro-Communist bourgeois literature of this period should be so strongly marked by speculations such as these is at least evidence of honourable intent. At this time it had somehow become obvious that the art most valued over the ages had been made at great human cost, and that to eliminate oppression was more important than to continue a tradition reserved for the privileged. This is the theme of Benjamin's most famous essay, and it was the preoccupation of many good writers. But, however compelling the theory, the practical problem remained difficult. The example of John Sommerfield comes to mind, author of *May Day* (1936), a novel displaying considerable technical resource in the interest of a sort of realism of the collectivity, an anti-bourgeois bourgeois novel. One can guess that the very skills he was aware of possessing seemed to this young writer to have been unjustly come by; that is the conviction which persuaded him that he must also use the kind of rhetoric familiar from Lewis Jones:

as he stands and watches he is caught up with the rhythm of the marching feet, he is filled with their strength and with gladness at the consciousness that he has thrown in his lot with their class and their party. For a long time he watches the faces going by, the thousands of faces, no two the same yet each stamped with something indefinable that is common to them all and different from those who stand and watch them from behind windows.[11]

This seems forced and doctrinaire, as the parallel in Jones isn't. It sounds all wrong in a book so much defter, more through-composed—more 'bourgeois'—than Jones's; and it is partly for that reason that it seems dated, trapped in its period, talking as not even modern Marxists would talk. That is doubtless the reason why the virtues of Sommerfield's book are largely forgotten along with its embarrassments. Steinbeck and Dos Passos are still read, but their reputations have waned, while Jones and Sommerfield are hardly read at all. We have set our faces against writing that has the marks of an avowed ideological commitment, especially if it leans to the left. If you look up these names in *The Oxford Companion to English Literature*: Lewis Jones, Walter Brierley, John Sommerfield, Alick West, Ralph Fox, Ralph Bates, Tom Wintringham, Julian Bell, you find that not one of them is included, though Walter Greenwood is—Ms Snee would doubtless say because he was a no-hoper, a

---

[11] *May Day* (1936; 1984 edn.), 241–2.

non-participant in the struggle, a servile collaborator with the bourgeois enemy.

This doesn't mean that Ms Drabble has been consciously submitting her authors to a political test; yet in the last analysis these exclusions are political, and they reflect the current state of educated taste.[12] By the same token the Marxist theorists of the time— Caudwell, West, Fox—attract little admiration even from their successors. And yet they are valuable witnesses to a remarkable moment in literary history, an attempt to unify bourgeois intellect and proletarian culture. It is almost embarrassing to say so; we have preferred to forget that moment. It confronts us with a problem we are virtually prevented by our own education from solving. How do we know that it is 'our' kind of writing that has most 'merit' and 'aesthetic value'? How dependent are these assumptions on the success of one class against another? Can we any longer imagine a culture in which Lewis Jones, despite his lack of 'merit', might be much more highly valued than the treasures of our own tradition? The left-wing bourgeois writers of the Thirties may have failed to answer these questions, but they were at least willing to take them on. But of course they supposed themselves to be on the brink of revolution, apocalypse; and that clears the mind wonderfully. As I remarked earlier, we have routinized apocalypse, and revolution always happens somewhere else, so in our role as posterity we feel pretty secure in our valuations and are not grateful to be reminded of the virtues of insecurity.

In the new Soviet state the need to adapt bourgeois art to proletarian uses—to give reasons for the preservation of works that were ideologically repugnant—was understood to be very urgent. Earlier Marxist literary theory had already established what might rather clumsily be called a principle of interpretative discrepancy —there could be a difference between what a work seemed meant to say and its actual socialist meaning, so that art produced under the old abhorrent dispensations now superseded could nevertheless serve the socialist cause. This theory accounts for the esteem in which Marx and Engels held Balzac, whose virtues could therefore

---

[12] Klaus, in the article cited, gives a bibliography of socialist fiction in the Thirties which has seventy-four titles. Of the authors listed only Hanley, Gibbon, Greenwood, Bates, Slater, Anand, Storm Jameson, Lindsay, and Halward are at all familiar today, even as names; and of the nine I mention only four (Anand, Gibbon, Greenwood, and Jameson) find a place in the *Oxford Companion*.

be affirmed later by the *Soviet Encyclopedia* and by Lukács. Engels had shown no more than a polite interest in realism and disliked the presence of overt political elements in art, where they might frighten bourgeois readers; the message, in his opinion, must inhere in the aesthetic structure.[13] Soviet pronouncements about socialist realism, though they appealed to the authority of Engels, were not content with this bourgeois-derived theory of value. What they called for was realism, the old bourgeois realism transformed into a socialist one.

The formula for socialist realism announced in 1934 at the First Soviet Writers' Congress required that 'truthful, historically concrete representation of reality in its revolutionary development' be combined with efforts to remould the workers ideologically 'in the spirit of socialism'.[14] There were disagreements about what this meant; the formula tried to avoid the excesses of *Proletkult* without falling into Trotskyite heresy; but no one doubted that it implied fidelity to the party line while, in practice, insisting the artists choose nineteenth-century models rather than anything 'Modernist'. The rejection of *Proletkult* inevitably led to dependence on a discrepancy theory; for *Proletkult* (echoed in England, as we have seen, by Alec Brown) had wanted a proletarian culture completely severed from bourgeois antecedents. To answer it one needed to claim that these antecedents, properly interpreted, could be heard to speak revolutionary truth.

The problem the Congress sought to solve was thus quite similar to that of the bourgeois Communists in the West: if you resisted the argument that the records of the wicked past ought to be junked, you had to find present uses for them. And you needed to claim that they could be read as freed by time from the old order. In so far as they represented it justly, they showed why socialism was necessary; and they could be read as typological anticipations of true socialism. To borrow the appropriate jargon, work which on the face of it did not exemplify socialist values might embody them 'objectively'. The value of such work obviously has to be ascertained by interpretation; what matters is not its original meaning but its application, or, as E. D. Hirsch would say, not its meaning but its significance. And of course such interpretation would be controlled by the Party.

[13] See P. Demetz, *Marx, Engels and the Poets* (1967), 128.
[14] Quoted in D. W. Fokkema and E. Kunne-Ibisch, *Theories of Literature in the Twentieth Century* (1977), 97.

Despite the complexities of these and subsequent deliberations they can be seen to offer paradigm instances of two related practices that seem essential to the business of literary evaluation: first, the salvation by interpretation of works that might otherwise have to be condemned as ideologically unacceptable; secondly, the selection and control of a literary canon by an institution. A bureaucracy will decide that Balzac and Tolstoy are in, Joyce and Proust out, as well as establishing the standards to be observed by current writers; and these decisions can if necessary be enforced by the police.

Much or most of the admired Russian literature since 1934 (so far as one can tell) has been produced by writers in revolt against socialist realism or, in the view of the authorities, getting it wrong. The conflict between the cultures of the classes seems, in this area, to be unending. It may be oversimple to say that behind the notion that Tolstoy and Balzac can be made to speak revolutionary truth there must be (as there was not among the adherents of *Proletkult*) a hidden belief in what Empson called 'permanent truths', which could be got into literature and could survive the obsolescence of a particular ideology. Thus we find no difficulty in telling students that, although the ideology of *Paradise Lost* is obsolete, we may, with proper study and instruction, understand that what it says about love, death, and history is not. Arguments of this sort may not be acceptable to abolitionists and proponents of catastrophic change; but it is interesting that they commended themselves, in one way or another, to the Party, even in the aftermath of political changes that could well be called catastrophic. For the Party accepted the value of past art, even if on the surface ideologically obsolete and repugnant.

What of more recent Marxist literary theory, no longer tied to the political emergencies of the Thirties, fully aware of discrepancies between the thought of that epoch and its own, and alert to a more modern context of literary theory? Has it found ways more congenial of saving for modern Marxism the literature of the past? I have time to consider in any detail only one critic, and choose him because he has seriously and directly addressed the question of value: I mean Terry Eagleton, the most fluent and engaging of our English neo-Marxist critics, and in particular his book *Criticism and Ideology* (1976). In the ten years since its publication Eagleton has written a lot more theory and criticism, and has qualified some of his earlier views, but I think by way of adjusting rather than of abandoning them; so much is suggested by the Preface to his most recent collection, *Against the Grain* (1986), though he is now critical of Althusser and shows a new interest in the relations of Marxism with Deconstruction and Feminism, together with an awareness of increased pressures from capitalism. Elsewhere he confesses his former uncritical acceptance of bourgeois definitions of literature as an autonomous practice; having eliminated this taint he has come to see the necessity of attacking the idea of a literary canon, arguing that 'literary criticism cannot justify its self-limiting to certain works by an appeal to their "value"' because it is 'part of a literary institution which constitutes these works as valuable in the first place'.[15] However, he does not seem to be saying that there is no literary value except as so constituted.

In *Criticism and Ideology* Eagleton presents a version of what I have been calling the discrepancy theory, arguing that texts can under Marxist analysis reveal a meaning not intended by the author. On this view what interests the analyst is the *non dit*; he works in the gaps of the text rather than in the text itself, practising what Althusser called 'symptomatic reading'. Taking the hint from psychoanalysis, he seeks to read absences as well as presences, working on distortions and unwilled omissions and so making contact with a subtext which is vaguely analogous to the unconscious. The implication is that the degree to which a text reveals its ideological basis under analysis is an indication of its value.

The task of criticism, on this view, is 'to show the text as it cannot know itself, to manifest those conditions of its making (inscribed in its very letter) about which it is necessarily silent. It is not just that the text knows some things and not others; it is rather that its very self-knowledge is the construction of a self-oblivion' (p. 43). This ignorant text knows no history, presenting in its place ideology. It offers nothing that can be called 'real'; its 'pseudo-real is the product of the ideologically saturated demands of its modes of representation' (p. 74), and it reveals what are called 'the categories of the lived' only in a concealed form (p. 76). To find what is concealed you must also study the aesthetic mode of concealment. It is the concealed that confers value.

In other words, nothing a work appears to be saying about its own ideological context is worthy of any notice except what may be

---

[15] *Literary Theory: An Introduction* (1983), 202.

necessary to its discounting. Criticism should concern itself less with what the work ostensibly presents than with the absences that make it incomplete—with what resides in an 'unconsciousness' of which the work itself cannot be aware. Eagleton won't quite go so far as to say that 'the work's identity is wholly constituted by what it is not' (p. 93); what one has to study is 'a complex series of transactions between text and ideology which are concealed by the apparent concreteness and naturalness of the text'; these the critic must penetrate 'to make its real determinants appear' (p. 101).

Applying these principles to particular texts, he finds, as one would expect, that the measures of autonomy conferred on texts by the bourgeois concept of organic form is merely part of the business of concealment. The idea of totality in works of art—which most criticism assumes in some form or other as a criterion of value—has always been a difficulty to Marxists; Adorno found his own solution, but apparently only for music. It is certainly not available as an instrument of valuation. How then should a Marxist critic deal with the problem of artistic value? He finds it less easy than his predecessors to concede, even by implication, that a text may have values which can be realized in quite different historical circumstances from those of its origin. What Eagleton maintains is that there is 'no value which is not *transitive*' (p. 166); value is produced in the act of reading, the (re)production of the text in a correct ideological context. It is the reader who effects those transactions between text and ideology.

In his need to avoid what seem the oversimplifications of earlier Marxist criticism Eagleton here comes close to painting himself into a corner. He agrees with Trotsky that a rootless populism is not the answer; nor is a historicism which makes too easy an equation of a work's world-view with that of a class; nor is formalism, which neglects history. Moreover he cannot help thinking that there is *some* quality which makes works of art works of art, not documents in the class war; and that art depends on something common to all, like death (as Trotsky remarked). Art moves us; it is not just a form of history; it cannot be reduced to the 'historico-ideological of which it is the product' (p. 177). The aesthetic speaks of its historical conditioning by not speaking of it. The value of Dante or of Yeats is not that they express their eras but that their ideological limitations provide the basis for their aesthetic achievements; the poetry of Yeats enables us to see the 'fault-lines' in its ideological formation (p. 181).

Sometimes Eagleton even seems to imply that the value of the work may be highest in just such cases because more productive of athwartness, complexity, significant dissonance, estrangement, and 'fault-lines'. So it isn't a question of making allowances for faulty ideology—the value of the work of art is said to *depend* on the exposure of the faults, and so on the faults themselves.

A fascinating and lengthy struggle with the problem of value, considered from a Marxist point of view, thus ends paradoxically by saving the value of past work even if—especially if—its ideology remains repugnant to the socialist conscience. This is a strange sophistication of the old Russian position, which maintained that a book might by application have value independent of the writer's false ideology. Other Marxists have found contradictions in Eagleton's position, blaming him for his anti-populism and his backdoor welcome to something like the Leavisian Great Tradition, so that, instead of doing what he hoped to do—eradicate bourgeois fallacies and correct Marxist errors—he has, it is claimed, only succeeded in upholding the myth of Literature 'as an abstract and eternal aesthetic category'.[16]

But the real difficulty seems to be that, for all its subtle provisions and interpretative athleticism, this theory of value depends finally on an institutionalized and authoritarian view of history. You can sort out the major from the minor by a consideration of the relations between the text, with its ideological fault-lines, and the true history to be seen through it. And, however you complicate this by stressing the complexity of these relations, in the end you have to have an authoritative view of what true history is, as distinct from false ideological versions of it. Or: since only Marxists have the truth about history and the ideological base which, with whatever degree of complexity, controls the value of the text, valuation is the privilege of Marxists; and, even if their valuations sometimes co-incide with those of non-Marxists, they alone are properly equipped to make them.

Fredric Jameson, an American Marxist critic much admired by Eagleton, endorses this magisterial position very candidly in *The Political Unconscious* (1981), declaring Marxism to be 'the untranscendable horizon' within which other critical methods exist, 'at once cancelling and preserving them' (p. 10), so that a Marxist can use the

---

[16] T. Bennett, *Formalism and Marxism* (1979), 155.

other methods as tools; but his main business is with the perception by means of the manifest text of the latent, the unconscious or subtext. Eagleton admires Jameson because he ingeniously tries to have it both ways, seeing no conflict between methods which depend on concepts of textual totality and a 'symptomal' attention to the discontinuities through which we peer into the unconscious.[17] Eagleton can't quite accept this, but Jameson is anticipating the charge that to treat the 'unconscious' of the text as the only matter of importance is dismayingly reductive. He quotes with approval some disparaging remarks of Deleuze and Guattari about Freudian interpretation—'a system of allegorical interpretation in which the data of one narrative line are radically impoverished by their rewriting according to the paradigm of another narrative, which is taken as the former's master-code or Ur-narrative and proposed as the ultimate hidden or unconscious *meaning* of the first one' (p. 22). Having understood this danger, Jameson is of course anxious to explain that he himself has not fallen into it—that his 'political unconscious' is not just such a 'master-code' or 'unconscious *meaning*'; and so, ostensibly swimming against the Marxist stream, he sets about devising legitimate ways of attending to the totality of the work, just as bourgeois critics do or did. That totality, he says, must be seen as

the rewriting or restructuration of a prior historical or ideological *subtext*, it being always understood that that 'subtext' is not immediately present as such, not some commonsense external reality, not even the conventional narratives of history manuals, but rather must itself be (re)constructed after the fact (p. 81).

The 're' in 'reconstructed' is in brackets, a fashionable device for having it both ways.

This Marxist theology (and its expression) may well strike you as excessively contorted—it certainly lacks the devotional simplicity of Marxist literary theory in the passionate Thirties. The illustrative exegesis can also be pretty complicated. Jameson demonstrates his method with a long analysis of *Lord Jim*, at the end of which he says quite cheerfully, 'But if this is what *Lord Jim* is really all about, then it only remains to ask why nobody thinks so, least of all Conrad himself' (p. 265). His answer to this question seems rather oblique, but I think we can see that the argument is another sophisticated

---

[17] *Against the Grain* (1986), p. 61.

version of what earlier discrepancy theorists maintained. However, Jameson holds that nobody before him had been able 'to restore the whole socially concrete subtext of late nineteenth-century rationalization and reification [he uses these terms from Weber and Lukács as equivalent] of which this novel is so powerfully . . . the expression and the Utopian compensation alike' (p. 266). And he is clear that one talks about the text only as a preliminary to talking about its whole historical constitution. The indissoluble connection of the text and history is now explained in terms remote from those of antecedent and more vulgar Marxisms, but values are still to be determined in accordance with an institutionalized version of history.

It is worth remarking that these critics rarely exercise themselves on works that the bourgeoisie would dismiss as trash. The structuralists used to do their stuff on James Bond, but Jameson prefers Balzac and Conrad, Stendhal and Wyndham Lewis. In this he is, like Eagleton, neo-Trotskyite as well as neo-Leavisite. Eagleton can call the literary canon a fiction invented by a literary institution which is 'part of the ideological apparatus of the modern capitalist state' and dedicated to the perpetuation of the illusion that literature is 'a distinct, bounded object of knowledge';[18] what prevents him from abandoning it altogether, in the manner proposed at the end of his book on literary theory, is precisely the problem of value. In the end he would change the canon or revalue its contents rather than do away with it.

As feminists are well aware, all attempts to impose new valuations have to fight against institutional prejudice. As we have seen, an instance of such prejudice is the persistent opposition to what looks like propaganda, which must be one reason why Eagleton and Jameson choose to write about Balzac and Conrad rather than Lewis Jones or John Sommerfield. Even they have, like most of us, a lingering liberal prejudice in favour of disinterest. This prejudice accounts for the suspicious attitude to much Thirties writing even in critics who might be expected to have got rid of it for good political reasons. Instead they find political reasons for placing high valuations on work that is already highly valued, though evidently not for the right reasons. It is curious that a much more revolutionary line is taken by the non-Marxist Stanley Fish, for whom all questions

---

[18] *Literary Theory: An Introduction*, pp. 200 ff.

of value would be questions about the procedures of what he calls
'interpretive communities'—crudely, that if some powerful advo-
cate could persuade those communities to attend to Lewis Jones
rather than to Shakespeare, Lewis Jones would be the more valuable
writer. The community decides what is literature and what isn't,
what is worth attention and what isn't; whoever has the power to
impose interpretations (and values) will determine them for the
community. Yet even Fish can be found calling a piece of writing
'fine', and he seems to have no more objection than most writers to
being thought valuable himself; he might say that this was a consen-
sual judgement issuing from some interpretative community, but it
has at least a smack of immanence.[19]

Granted, then, that some element of literary value is at least as-if
immanent, what is the importance of that historical context into
which works held not to be valuable tend to disappear, while those
that are held to be valuable survive either in spite of it or because they
are successful in exposing its ideological unacceptability? When does
value survive the historical moment of the work, and when not?
Suppose our community has a consensus that Jones is not much read
because his novels are to an unacceptable degree dated propaganda.
Somebody might then come along and claim that this judgement is
based on a misunderstanding of the period—that there is particular
interest, and so a particular value, in the record of a quite exceptional
conflict between on the one hand the old notions of disinterest, and
the desirability of what Benjamin called aura, and on the other the
immediate demands of politics and conscience—a conflict expressed
by the Congress of Soviet Writers in one way, by W. H. Auden in
another, and by Lewis Jones in yet another. Good transactions
between text and context depend upon one's getting the context
more or less right, and in neglecting the sense of urgency that was
common in Thirties writers (though not in us) we may be getting the
context wrong.

A simpler notion of the complexity of the problem can perhaps be
got from considering the ideological formation of a book all parties,
short-circuiting their various judicial procedures, would allow to
be trash. I have long thought that detective stories and thrillers are
the best place to look if you want to find ideologies lying around
uncriticized, prejudices innocently stated as facts. So when I thought

[19] *Is there a Text in this Class?* (1980), 135.

an example of this sort of thing would be useful at the end of this chapter I picked up the example of the genre that happened to lie nearest to hand. It was an early novel by Agatha Christie called *The Secret Adversary* (1922). (I note, by the way, that the *Oxford Companion* extols her 'matchless ingenuity' and 'her ear for dialogue', so it was perhaps hasty of me to say 'all parties'.) There is a Prologue in which a man accosts a girl on the sinking *Lusitania*; having carefully ascertained that she is a patriotic American, he entrusts to her some vital secret papers. (He has no choice of sex, since women, he supposes, will get into the lifeboats and men won't.) It is the post-war fate of these papers that animates the plot of the novel proper. A nice young ex-officer, unemployed and broke, teams up with a bright girl—they address each other as 'old bean' and 'old thing'—and they get involved in a search for the vital papers. It is essential that these should not come to light, for if they did so an important statesman (Tory) would be discredited. Unscrupulously used, they might even help Labour to win a general election, and that would constitute 'a grave disability to English trade'. Even as it is, the nation is tormented by labour unrest, directly attributable to 'Bolshevist gold . . . pouring into this country for the specific purpose of procuring a Revolution'. The mastermind behind the plot to use the secret papers is, shamefully enough, an Englishman, 'pro-German, as he would have been pro-Boer', and unfortunately 'the finest criminal brain of the age'.

The assistants of this villain are a cosmopolitan crew, some of them fit only for the pages of Lombroso. One is 'obviously of the very dregs of society. The low beetling brows, and the criminal jaw, the bestiality of the whole countenance' demonstrate that he is 'of a type that Scotland Yard would have recognized at a glance'. Another is a German ('if that isn't a Hun, I'm a Dutchman,' muses the young man) and another 'an obvious Sinn Feiner'. The Russians are especially villainous ('In Russia we have ways of making a girl talk') and luxurious (one of them wears a fur coat: 'Fur lined? And you a Socialist!').

When the action is over, the mastermind foiled, and the politician's reputation saved, there is a labour demonstration in London. In this chapter I have already quoted two accounts of such marches, and the literature of the time contains many more; but this march is not a bit like those of Jones and Sommerfield. 'The 29th, the much-heralded "Labour Day", has passed much as any other day.'

A few speeches in the Park and Trafalgar Square, some aimlessly straggling processions singing 'The Red Flag'—that was all. Newspapers which had hinted at a general strike followed by a reign of terror 'were forced to hide their diminished heads'. Labour leaders were embarrassed, the Government conciliatory: 'England was saved!' And it was decided that the guilt of the eminent English traitor must never be revealed. 'Sir James's long association with the law would make it undesirable.'

Perhaps in this case we can all spot some of those typological anticipations which are said to give value to old books. We may first ask whether there is anything ironical about the tone of these concluding pages. Of course there isn't. Everything, including the intense chauvinism, is a naïve reflection of unexamined ideological assumptions. The year 1921 had been one of depression, of strikes and threats of strikes, of war in Ireland, Communist riots, hyperinflation in Germany, and so on. None of this intrudes into the post-war scene of Agatha Christie's novel. Patriotism is an English (and by extension an American) virtue, Sir James being a notable exception, corrupted by his interest in a criminal world full of foreigners and degenerates, and possibly also by his intelligence. The English working class is represented as quite happy to kill Bolsheviks, and it is not even mentioned that some of them at the docks degenerately refused to load arms for the White Russians. The upper classes are shown to be humorous and tenacious, though not as clever or as rich as their American counterparts. The poor are those from whom one keeps things it is better for them not to have or to know. Politically, the mood is rather like that which a couple of years later produced the Zinoviev letter, an attempt to prevent the disaster of a Labour victory in the General Election. This is in terms of its social representations a much more elaborately wrought novel than Dame Agatha was later accustomed to write,[20] and the consequence is that there are farcically numerous fissures or fault-lines through which we can discern its productive ideology, which of course comes through in the text simply as a set of norms of decent behaviour. I imagine the only reason one could give for refusing it a full-scale Eagletonian analysis would be that it is obviously

[20] The nice young man and the bright girl recur in later novels of Dame Agatha, and seem to have had devoted admirers. They age suitably, and the ideological context becomes less dense, but so far as I can tell the novels in which they appear are among the less fascinating of the œuvre.

valueless. But how can one tell without looking through its gaps?

I agree that to carry on like this about an innocent thriller is a bit heavy-handed, though it does some butterflies good to be broken on wheels. And the relation of texts to historical ideologies is a matter of importance, greatly complicating this question of value. Another complication is the way in which we mythologize or even falsify history in order to make easier the task of assessing works produced at this or that historical period. I shall be discussing that in the next chapter.

6 · Canon and Period

Notions of value in literature more often than not involve, as a rule rather obscurely, our views of the relation of a work to its historical context. We have seen that for some that relation is simple and extremely intimate; they would argue that the best contemporary valuation is the one that ought to be preserved by the tradition as it is maintained by Anthony Savile's 'core of persons who give the culture its character'.

They believe that the best interpretation, on which valuation must depend, seeks the original intention of the author, and that valuations which ignore it and consider instead the later or applied senses of an old work—proceed, as some put it, in terms of its significance rather than its meaning—are at least less authentic or inauthentic. There are those, like the Marxists, who hold in some form the view that the work may in its later existence have value that was not evident in its original form, the passage of time having made available its true relation to a necessarily false ideology enshrined in it. And there are many variations on this belief in a manageable discrepancy between the work as it was and the work as it now is, in a later historical phase, most of them confiding in the power of later readers to discern what for them is the true value of a work conceived in a remote historical situation which they can only approach from their own historical situation, without seeking an impossible identification with the prejudices and expectations of an original audience. One such is the historical approach we associate with the hermeneutic theory of Gadamer. What seems true of all such approaches, and what distinguishes them all from the anarchic or nihilistic attitude which would abolish the old work along with the past as a whole, is that they all assume the need to account for the relation between the value of a work and its relation to the historical context not only of the work but of its interpreters and assessors. Judgements of value, from abolitionism to the latest elaborations of Marxism, cannot possibly avoid assumptions about the operations of history.

It seems necessary, therefore, to say something rather general and elementary about the ways in which history is manipulated in the interests of literary valuation. There seem to be two main ways in which we try to make history manageable for literary purposes: by making canons that are in some sense transhistorical; and by inventing historical periods. They enable us to package historical data that would otherwise be hopelessly hard to deal with; and they do so by making them *modern*.

That history is a construct, that even the most positivist of historians is not content with, and in any case cannot achieve, a record of simple successiveness, a chronicle without a *telos*; and that the historian's sense of that end will be determined by his own historical position: these are commonplace propositions, and in one form or another have been so for a couple of centuries. In his inaugural lecture at Jena in 1789 Schiller distinguished between events and their history, adding, to quote Lionel Gossman's paraphrase, that 'the historian's perception is determined by his own situation, so that events are often torn out of the dense and complex web of their contemporary relations in order to be set in a pattern constructed retrospectively by the historian'.[1] And it had long been understood that 'every attempt to devise an order different from that of pure chronicle involved an appeal to the order of art—of fictional narrative or drama'.[2] Later philosophers of history developed this idea to the point where it became a problem to distinguish between history and fiction.[3] Yet, as Gossman remarks, the appetite for the real, which requires an acceptance of the construct as a natural occurrence, remains even more stubbornly strong in history than in fiction; and it is the habit of many historians to do what they can to satisfy it.

For example, no historical slogan is more often quoted than Ranke's 'wie es eigentlich bewesen' of which the usual translation, endlessly quoted, states that history should show what actually happened. But an at least equally correct translation would be 'how, essentially, things happened'. Stephen Bann examines the implications of this ambiguity of translation in his original and lively book *The Clothing of Clio* (1984). In the more familiar version Ranke's

[1] L. Gossman, 'History and Literature,' in R. H. Canary and H. Kozicki (eds.), *The Writing of History: Literary Form and Historical Understanding* (1978), 3–39; p. 19.
[2] Ibid. 20.
[3] See especially R. G. Collingwood, *The Idea of History* (1946), and W. B. Gallie, *Philosophy and the Historical Understanding* (1964). The literature on the subject is very extensive, and the following books might also be mentioned: A. C. Danto, *Analytic Philosophy of History* (1968), M. White, *Foundations of Historical Knowledge* (1965), and H. White, *Metahistory* (1973).

dictum stands as the motto of a positivist historiography he would not himself have endorsed, and which nobody could really believe except when under the spell of a myth of realism. Facts are not events, and history deals with events and plots. The notion that we can present Clio naked, without structural support and without the integument of rhetoric, is unacceptable. It would be a form of writing without *parti pris*, without presuppositions governing the selection of evidence, without attributions of cause, without structure, without style, and without end. There is no such degree zero. Bann examines some of the ways in which the goddess stays modest. As Wallace Stevens's Ozymondias observed, 'The bride | Is never naked. A fictive covering | Weaves always glistening from the heart and mind'.

Here is a simple example, drawn, in the spirit of the discussion in the previous chapter about miners and strikes, from A. J. P. Taylor's account of the General Strike of 1926. He is talking about the response of other workers to the call for a national strike:

The response of union members was fantastic: all ceased work when called upon, and practically none returned to work until the strike was over. These were the very men who had rallied to the defence of Belgium in 1914. The voluntary recruitment of the first World War and the strike of 1926 were acts of spontaneous generosity, without parallel in any other country. The first was whipped on by almost every organ of public opinion; the second was undertaken despite their disapproval. Such nobility deserves more than a passing tribute. The strikers asked nothing for themselves. They did not seek to challenge the government, still less to overthrow the constitution. They merely wanted the miners to have a living wage. Perhaps not even that. They were loyal to their unions and to their leaders, as they had been. loyal during the war to their country and to their generals. They went once more into the trenches, without enthusiasm and with little hope.[4]

Here the historian is expressing his own opinion that the behaviour of the union members was generous and noble, and associating their disinterested support of the miners with their readiness to go to the defence of Belgium in 1914. This connecting of two disparate

---

[4] A. J. P. Taylor, *English History, 1914–1945* (The Oxford History of England, 15; 1965), 244–45. My attention has been drawn to the analysis of a paragraph from Taylor's *The Course of German History* by Hayden White in his *Tropics of Discourse* (1978) in which White shows how a simple historical statement 'has a secondary sense' arising from a constructive process, poetic in nature, which is added to the representation of historical fact.

historical events enables him at the end of the paragraph to conflate them rhetorically; in joining the strike they were going once more into the trenches, this time even more nobly because without popular support and without personal enthusiasm. He gives as a justification for this boldness of metaphor his opinion that the workers deserve more than a passing tribute. Of course there is a factual basis for what he is doing, since there are presumably statistics which show that 'all ceased work' and that 'practically none returned to work before the strike was over'. If we were very pedantic and very positivist we might ask for evidence that the sympathetic strikers were the same people who volunteered in 1914; and we might complain that the historian takes account neither of the fact that by 1926 lots of those volunteers were dead, nor of the fact that only men over twenty-six were old enough to have been in the wartime army. But in fact we don't quibble like this, partly because we know he is speaking of miners less as individuals than as a corporate body that persists as it were timelessly, but also because we know very well that historians, like non-Modernist novelists, usually feel free to have opinions and even emotions; just as works of fiction need not consist entirely of fictional discourse, works of history need not consist entirely of historical discourse, and may well contain expressions of opinion, compassion, distaste, etc., of the sort often to be found in works of fiction.[5] In this case, for instance, we note a certain wonder at the altruism of the workers, treated in the pastoral mode as if they were *others*, members of an admirable but alien culture.

The only powerful constraint habitually felt by writers of history (if we leave out of account the refined strictures of philosophers of history) is the reader's set of expectations. These include an expectation of connexity and relevance and a requirement, only apparently simple and in fact very complex, that this is how things essentially were. They also include an expectation that the historian may well see connections between such disparate events as the war and the strike, and may well find in that connection occasion to praise the nobility of the strikers, and use metaphor to join the war and the strike unexpectedly together by a rhetorical device which will enable him to render that nobility the more movingly or persuasively.

[5] I adapt this formula from J. R. Searle's essay 'The Logical Status of Fictional Discourse', in his *Expression and Meaning* (1979), 74.

This amounts to saying that we don't in fact like history to be what Acton said it ought to be, critical and colourless; we accept without much question a measure of mythmaking, the intrusion of personal feeling, or, it may be, nationalist or class feeling. Of course there are different kinds of history, each with its own peculiar conditions, but we should expect most of these general provisions to obtain for all: there will be patterns, causes, events rather than mere facts, opinions rather than flat chronicles, clothes for Clio.

How does literary history fare in these circumstances? For the past quarter-century or so a rumour has circulated to the effect that it can't any longer be written. Causal connections between works chosen for attention must be spurious, and special interests, not strictly literary at all, guide the historian's hand. Yet, as Hans Robert Jauss remarks, it used to be thought that the crowning achievement of the philologist was to write the history of his national literature, to reveal its origins with pride, and to trace its stately and inevitable development. These interests in origins and development received a great fillip at the Renaissance, and they flourished well into the present century. But it then began to seem obvious that something was wrong, and that historians of literature were actually writing histories not of literature but of other things—treating literature as a set of illustrative documents, smuggling in notions of cause and connection from social and political history.[6]

The esteem in which Jauss is currently held is due to his abandonment of the old ways of arranging the data 'according to general tendencies, genres, and what-have-you, in order to treat within these rubrics the individual works in chronological series', endorsing canonical valuations by establishing a quasi-causal relation between the big authors. He wants a literary history which is a history of reception, open-ended because reception (and valuation) are always in progress. He dislikes the practice of separating the big names from what Curtius called 'the tradition of mediocrity' and talking about them as if they were independent of the action of time, transcending the history in which the less valued are stuck. He distrusts the Formalists with their doctrine of 'estrangement'—the devices by which a work is foregrounded against the conventions of its time —because that road leads straight back into conventional non-

---

[6] See R. Wellek and A. Warren, *Theory of Literature* (1949), 263, and R. Wellek, 'The Fall of Literary History', in *The Attack on Literature* (1982), 64–77, for a survey of the present situation.

literary history. To correct this error he thinks it necessary to combine the Formalist insights with those of post-Heideggerian hermeneutics; by such means he can hope to be rid of 'historical objectivism' and instead study reception 'within the objectifiable system of expectations that arises from each work in the historical moment of its appearance, from a pre-understanding of the genre . . . and from the opposition between poetic and practical language'. Thus the historian can try to create a 'horizon of expectations', and institute communication between that horizon and his own, as in Gadamer's 'fusion of horizons'.[7]

I don't think this method can eliminate the prejudice that decides major and minor, or even what is literature and what isn't, and Jauss does retain a notion of canonicity (which must be to some extent prejudiced) and a fairly distinct notion of period, now made more subtle by its refinement into a horizon, but still involving a preselection of material and even of the kinds of thing one can say about a work that lies within that period. But this is a more subtle model for literary historians than most, even if it does not settle the problem of value, and even if it does not eliminate those myths, useful or dangerous according to your own prejudices, of canon and period. I shall now look at them in turn, though when I come to the question of period I shall say very little about the Modernist and Post-modernist periods, reserving them for the final chapter.

I can best start this section on canon by reading an item from the US *Chronicle of Higher Education* dated 4 September 1985. This journal is widely circulated in American institutions of higher education. On this occasion, at the beginning of a new academic year, it ran a symposium in which twenty-two authorities in various fields told readers what developments to expect over the next few years. This is the forecast for literary studies:

The dominant concern of literary studies during the rest of the nineteen-eighties will be literary theory. Especially important will be the use of theory informed by the work of the French philosopher Jacques Derrida to gain insights into the cultures of blacks and women.
    In fact the convergence of feminist and Afro-American theoretical formulations offers the most challenging nexus for scholarship in the coming years. Specifically the most exciting and insightful accounts of expressive

---

[7] H. R. Jauss, *Toward an Aesthetic of Reception*, trans. T. Bahi (1982), 3–45.

culture in general and creative writing in particular will derive from efforts
that employ feminist and Afro-American approaches to the study of texts by
Afro-American writers such as Zora Neale Hurston, Sonia Sanchez, Gloria
Naylor and Toni Morrison.

Among the promising areas for analysis is the examination of the concerns
and metaphorical patterns that are common to past and present black
women writers.

Such theoretical accounts of the cultural products of race and gender will
help to undermine the half-truths that white males have established as
constituting American culture as a whole. One aspect of that development
will be the continued reshaping of the literary canon as forgotten, neglected
or suppressed texts are re-discovered.

Literary theory is also full of disruptive and deeply political potential,
which Afro-American and feminist critics will labor to release in coming
years.

This manifesto, for such it appears to be, was written by the
Professor 'of English and of Human Relations' at the University of
Pennsylvania. It proposes what could well be called a radical deconstruction of the canon, putting in the place of the false elements
foisted into it by white males a list of black females. These will be
studied by methods specifically Afro-American. The writer points
out the political implications of these developments, for he knows
that the changes he prophesies will not come to pass without
alterations in more than the syllabus. He assumes that the literary
canon is a load-bearing element of the existing power structure, and
believes that by imposing radical change on the canon you can help
to dismantle the power structure.

What interests me most about this programme is not its cunning
alliance of three forces that might be thought to be in principle hostile
to the idea of the canon—Feminism, Afro-Americanism, and Deconstruction—so much as its tacit admission that there is such a
thing as literature and that there ought to be such a thing as a canon;
the opinions of the powerful about the contents of these categories
may be challenged, but the concepts of themselves remain in place.
Indeed the whole revolutionary enterprise simply assumes their
continuance. The canon is what the insurgents mean to occupy as the
reward of success in the struggle for power.

In short, what we have here is not a plan to abolish the canon but
one to capture it. The association of canon with authority is deeply
ingrained in us, and one can see simple reasons why it should be so. It
is a highly selective instrument, and one reason why we need to use it

is that we haven't enough memory to process everything. The only other option is not a universal reception of the past and its literature but a Dadaist destruction of it. It must therefore be protected by those who have it and coveted by those who don't.

Authority has invented many myths for the protection of the canon. Religious canons can be effectively closed, even at the cost of retaining within them books of which the importance is later difficult to discern, like some of the briefer New Testament letters. They can be heavily protected, credited for example with literal inspiration, so that it is forbidden to alter one jot or tittle of them, diacritical signs, instructions to cantilators, even manifest errors. And every word, every letter, is subject to minute commentary. Whatever is included is sure to have its effect on the world. Suppose, for instance, that Revelation had not got into the Christian canon, as it almost didn't; it would have been just one more lost or apocryphal apocalypse, the province only of specialist scholarship; instead it has had vast effects on social and political behaviour over many ages, and continues to do so. The Fourth Gospel was at one time under suspicion; had it not become so central a document for Christian theology millions of people would have been required to believe something quite different from the orthodox faith, and quite a lot of them might have escaped burning if not burnt for some other reason.

So canons are complicit with power; and canons are useful in that they enable us to handle otherwise unmanageable historical deposits. They do this by affirming that some works are more valuable than others, more worthy of minute attention. Whether their value is wholly dependent on their being singled out in this way is a contested issue. There is in any case a quite unmistakable difference of status between canonical and uncanonical books, however they got into the canon. But once they are in certain changes come over them. First, they are completely locked into their times, their texts as near frozen as devout scholarship can make them, their very language more and more remote. Secondly, they are, paradoxically, by this fact, set free of time. Thirdly, the separate constituents become not only books in their own right but part of a larger whole—a whole because it is so treated. Fourthly, that whole, with all its interrelated parts, can be thought to have an inexhaustible potential of meaning, so that what happens in the course of time—as the original context and language of the collection grows more and more distant—is that new meanings accrue (they may be deemed, by a

fiction characteristic of this way of thinking, to be original meanings) and these meanings constantly change though their source
remains unchangeable. Since all the books can now be thought of as
one large book, new echoes and repetitions are discovered in remote
parts of the whole. The best commentary on any verse is another
verse, possibly placed very far away from it. This was a rabbinical
doctrine: 'I join passages from the Torah with passages from the
Hagiographa, and the words of the Torah glow as the day they were
given at Sinai.'[8]

The temporal gap between text and comment or application
ensures that in practice something like the Gadamer–Jauss hermeneutics, whether formalized or not, is always needed. The mutual
influence of one canonical text on another, intemporal in itself,
appearing in time only by means of commentary, is the essence of
Eliot's idea of a canon, expressed in that famous passage in the essay
'Tradition and the Individual Talent'—'the whole of the literature of
Europe . . . has a simultaneous existence and composes a simultaneous order', though he provides, as a secular canonist must, for
additions to that order: 'The existing monuments form an ideal order
among themselves, which is modified by the introduction of the new
(the really new) work of art among them.'[9] By this means 'order'
—timeless order—'persists after the supervention of novelty', and it
does so by adjusting itself to the new. Here the idea of canon is used
in the service of an order which can be discerned in history but
actually transcends it, and makes everything timeless and modern.

In this, as in the formulae of hermeneutics, in the rabbinical
methodology and in the Marxist aspirations toward a theory of
fruitful discrepancy, there is a clear purpose of making a usable past,
a past which is not simply past but also always new. The object of all
such thinking about the canonical monuments, then, is to make
them *modern*. Indeed variants of this view are found in more than one
writer of the period we now think of as 'Modernist'. At the same
time there was a rival kind of Modernism that professed a desire to
destroy the monuments, to destroy the past. But the ghost of
canonicity haunts even these iconoclasts. And whether one thinks of
canons as objectionable because formed at random or to serve some
interests at the expense of others, or whether one supposes that the

[8] D. Patte, *Early Jewish Hermeneutic in Palestine* (1975), 44.
[9] *Selected Prose of T. S. Eliot*, ed. F. Kermode (1975), 38.

contents of canons are providentially chosen, there can be no doubt that we have not found ways of ordering our thoughts about the history of literature and art without recourse to them. That is why the minorities who want to be rid of what they regard as a reactionary canon can think of no way of doing so without putting a radical one in its place.

This is true even if one agrees with Benjamin that 'there is no document of civilization which is not at the same time a document of barbarism',[10] for every 'document of civilization' retains qualities that set it apart from possible substitutes 'in an age of mechanical reproduction'; and to Benjamin, with his unmatched sense of their qualities (which he subsumes under the name of 'aura'), the abolition of such documents was close to unthinkable. He believed that the historical materialist should in conscience dissociate himself from these works of art, indissolubly associated in their making and in their transmission with injustice and oppression, but he was no more able to do so that the materialists I've already talked about, including those who believed that the works of art in question should be preserved as the dearly bought heritage of the descendants of the victims. Benjamin approved of Proust, with his sense of aura, of 'the incalculable individual life'[11] (a rather bourgeois expression, surely), and he disapproved of Dada, which would destroy both aura and the past. There is no escaping it: if we want the monuments, the documents we value, we must preserve them in spite of their evil associations, and find ways of showing that their value somehow persists in our changed world. Moreover we cannot avoid seeing them as interrelated, as of the same family by reason of their distinctive features and qualities. So we have somehow to place them in relation to one another; and the way we do that will help to determine our attitude to the past. The canon, in predetermining value, shapes the past and makes it humanly available, accessibly modern.

In earlier chapters I referred freely to the Thirties, betraying no fear that it might seem odd that a stretch of ten years could be assumed to connote a *period* and a *style* of writing and thinking that we can recognize and argue about. Some decades are graced in this way

---

[10] W. Benjamin, *Illuminations*, trans. H. Zohn (1968), 258.
[11] Ibid. 210.

—the Nineties is an obvious example; and the practice seems to be common in popular culture, for everybody now seems to have a clear and distinct idea of the Fifties and the Sixties. Periodization by decades is part of our familiar mental habit—another way of ordering the past (and so making it accessible to valuation). And this is the function also of grander concepts of period.

Periodization is a large and curious subject, and there is a big difference between scholarly discussion of it and the relatively careless way we talk about periods in our ordinary conversation. For instance, we might well use an expression such as 'post-Enlightenment thought' or whatever, and assume the term to be self-explanatory. I look up the word 'Enlightenment' in the *Oxford English Dictionary*, hoping to find a definition of this ordinary sense, with the expectation that the definition will be bolstered by reference to more cautious scholarly usage. What I do in fact find is the statement that the word is used 'to designate the spirit and aims of the French philosophers of the 18c., or of others whom it is intended to associate with them in the implied charge of shallow and pretentious intellectualism, unreasonable contempt for tradition and authority, etc.'. Two examples are appended, one from J. H. Stirling's book on Hegel (1865) ('Deism, Atheism, Pantheism, and all manner of *isms* due to Enlightenment', followed by 'shallow Enlightenment'); and the other from Edward Caird's book on Kant (1889): 'The individualistic tendencies of the age of Enlightenment . . .' This seems inadequate, especially if one recalls that in 1784 Kant wrote an essay called 'An Answer to the Question: What is Enlightenment?' ['*Was ist Aufklärung?*'] in which he expressly says that its chief feature is 'the escape of men from their self-incurred tutelage', the free public use of one's reason, adding that his age was making progress in that direction, thanks in part to the liberal policies of Frederick the Great; they were enlightening themselves, though by no means entitled to call theirs an Enlightened age.[12] Kant speaks as if a very large movement was in progress, and movements easily turn into periods; but to the *OED* the term Enlightenment suggests nothing but a late-eighteenth-century pseuds' corner. However, you may at this point charitably recall that 'E' is an early letter, compiled the best part of a century ago; so we must check the word in the *Supplement*, of

[12] Reprinted in D. Simpson (ed.), *German Aesthetic and Literary Criticism: Kant, Fichte, Schelling, Schopenhauer, Hegel*, (1984), 29–34.

which the relevant volume was published in 1972. But the *Supplement* has nothing to add under 'Enlightenment', and you may have to conclude that historically, as well as in common usage, 'Enlightenment' is a blanket expression covering various French, and judging by the examples also German, isms, which have only to be named to be despised.[13]

Ism is indeed a fiery particle; it can add or take away value, suggest adulation or disparagement—it all depends on how the user feels about novelty. And period descriptions have the same ambivalent quality, quite often starting life as sneer words and then being converted by other users into eulogisms. I suppose the classic instance is 'Baroque'. The derivation of the term seems uncertain, but its first use was disparaging; art historians used it to signify a period of relative decadence after the Renaissance. Burckhardt used 'baroque' or 'rococo' to signify the decadence of any style, using the supposed decadence of the post-Renaissance period as an archetype. 'Baroque' was given wide circulation by Wölfflin, who invented the celebrated distinction between 'closed' (Renaissance) and 'open' (Baroque) form, and was also the first writer to apply the term 'Baroque' to literature. In a celebrated passage in his book *Renaissance and Baroque* (1888) he called Ariosto 'Renaissance' and Tasso 'Baroque', explaining the distinction thus: Ariosto shares 'that wonderful intimacy of emphatic response to every single form that was characteristic of the Renaissance', but Tasso has the defects typical of Baroque, 'no sense of the significance of individual forms, only of the more muted effect of the whole'. As a description and evaluation of two styles, obviously related yet obviously different, this formula has some merit; but of course the valuations and stylistic descriptions of the two poets are transferred to the two successive historical periods, the point being to disparage Baroque. Wölfflin does not fully explain how one turned into the other, though he does venture to suggest that Jesuit Counter-Reformation piety had something to do with it, and this partial explanation came to be quite generally accepted.[14] René Wellek's well-known examination of 'Baroque' as

[13] It is only fair to add that there is an entry under *Aufklärung* which says the term describes 'a European intellectual movement in the 18th c. laying claim to extraordinary intellectual illumination and enlightenment'. This still leaves a lot to be said.

[14] *Renaissance and Baroque* (1888; trans. K. Simon, 1964), 83 ff. It is not accepted by C. J. Friedrich in *The Age of Baroque, 1610–1660* (1952); Friedrich thinks it altogether too limiting, and offers what is probably the most spectacular expansion of the

a literary term suggests that it hardly entered general use until the
1920s, when it was perhaps thought to offer a useful historical
parallel to the Expressionism then in vogue; and thereafter the term
was used more and more widely and more and more vaguely.[15] In
the Anglo-American tradition the only name firmly associated with
Baroque in the early stages of the development of that term was that
of Crashaw, which seems reasonable; but once established as a
eulogistic description its use was soon extended much beyond
religious fervour of a Jesuit kind. Here are some of the English
writers who have for one reason or another been described as
'Baroque' (usually, it must be said, by European critics and historians): Lyly, Shakespeare, Ben Jonson, Donne, Massinger, Ford,
Browne, Jeremy Taylor, Dryden, Giles and Phineas Fletcher,
Milton, Bunyan, Otway, Thomson, Collins, and Wordsworth.
As a stylistic description it simply floated free, whether you liked
whatever you were talking about or not.

    As the period style came to be thought valuable in itself, there
arose a need for further discrimination, and 'Mannerism' was in-
serted as an intermediate period between Renaissance and Baroque.
Like Baroque it was at first dyslogistic; in the nineteenth century it
was used of such unfavoured artists as Bronzino; but after 1920
(according to the OED Supplement) it served as a non-pejorative description of Italian art in the period 1500–1520. There seems to have
been some disagreement as to whether Mannerism was to be thought
of as a kind of hangover from the Renaissance or as the precursor of
Baroque; but as a period it is now accepted as something we cannot
get on without; yet it was entirely unknown to Wölfflin, for instance
(who would have called Baroque what is now thought of as
Mannerist).

    In his European Literature and the Latin Middle Ages Ernst Curtius
spends some time castigating wanton periodizers. 'Is Baudelaire

meaning of Baroque; for him it embraces politics, economics, philosophy, and
science as well as music, art, and literature. Rejecting Mannerism altogether, he
argues that the Baroque period extends from the middle of the sixteenth century to the middle
of the eighteenth century, a 'common field of feeling . . . focused on movement,
tension, force' and finding its 'richest fulfilment in the castle and the opera', as well as
the wig. Among the poets Milton, Shakespeare in the great tragedies and 'the idyllic
romances', and Jonson in the masques mingle with Lope de Vega, Calderón,
Góngora, and Corneille (1962 edn. 39–40, 47–61).

[15] R. Wellek, 'The Concept of Baroque in Literary Scholarship', in Concepts of
Criticism (1963), 69–127.

Impressionist, George Expressionist? Much intellectual energy is expended upon such problems,' he says. But on the same page he speaks of 'Baroque (i.e. Mannerism)' and later of 'late antique and medieval Mannerism'; and finally he sets up a polar opposition between Mannerism and Classicism, saying that Mannerism is not simply a period of art history but a 'manner' of 'overrunning the classical norm', constantly found in European literature. He then gives instances of Mannerist breaches of Classical norms through the ages—in Martial, Pliny, Ambrose, Góngora, Gracián, Mallarmé, and Joyce, declaring that Mannerism is far more useful as a conceptual instrument than the more familiar antithesis to Classicism, namely Romanticism, and certainly more useful than Baroque, which in his opinion ought to be liquidated.[16] Thus a quite modest notion is apotheosized, and virtually the whole of European literature pays tribute to it.

It appears, then, that concepts of period not only make history manageable but inevitably involve valuation; so that the characteristics thought to confer value (or its opposite) can be sought anywhere, with the object of making further valuations based upon a period archetype. Nevertheless that archetype remains in place, and what is said about a period style is deeply involved with one's apprehension of the period itself, more generally considered. This can easily be seen from the way in which the term 'Renaissance' is used. It may be surprising that everybody got along so well without it for so long; Huizinga finds the earliest example of its conversational use in a story by Balzac published in 1829.[17] In 1855 Michelet published a book entitled *The Renaissance*; five years later came Burckhardt's *The Civilisation of the Renaissance in Italy*. Because there were people living at the time of the Renaissance who supposed themselves to be assisting at a rebirth of ancient civilization, Panofsky, in what remains the most authoritative treatment of the subject, asks whether in so believing they were defining themselves or deceiving themselves; and E. H. Gombrich wonders whether we should not think of the Renaissance more as a movement than as a period.[18] But,

[16] E. Curtius, *European Literature and the Latin Middle Ages*, trans. W. R. Trask (1953), 12, 66, 273.
[17] Quoted in E. Panofsky, *Renaissance and Renascences in Western Art* (1960; 1969 edn.), 5.
[18] E. H. Gombrich, 'The Renaissance – Period or Movement?' in J. B. Trapp (ed.), *Background to the English Renaissance* (1974), 9–30.

although periods are often detected long after they are over, it is not unusual for people to think they are actually in one; such is the case with the 'Postmodernism' of the present moment. Movements can turn into periods, and Panofsky accepts the Renaissance (distinguishing it from mere 'renascences' like the lesser classical revivals of the tenth and twelfth centuries) as a 'megaperiod'.

Most of us believe in the Renaissance, though we have been taught to be cautious: the period wasn't characterized only by revival —there were profound misunderstandings both of antiquity and of the intervening period between antiquity and the present which was labelled 'the Middle Ages'.[19] And, as Panofsky remarks, even those who profess not to believe in it behave as if they do, especially when they want to disparage it. Valuations of the Renaissance vary from detestation—Ruskin, Worringer, Hulme, and Ezra Pound—to the more general commonplace eulogy. The dating of the period is vague: it has a plausible starting-point in Petrarch, and it might be said that Vasari's sense of a decadence marks its end; but in England the period still conventionally includes Shakespeare and even Milton, who, as we've seen, are also claimed for Baroque. Still, as Panofsky remarks, there are obvious differences between a Gothic cathedral and St Peter's; and it is not too extravagant to add that the first preaches Christian humility and the second is more interested in proclaiming the dignity of man, whether you think that was a good move or not.[20]

Once a period has got itself established we can not only argue about whether it ever existed in the way people habitually say it did, but use it very freely to scan history and make judgements of particular styles, and particular works, of art. This goes on despite all the judicious qualifications made by the scholars. The Renaissance was only one aspect of sixteenth-century culture, say Huizinga; we should be careful about the way we use such terms as 'Baroque', says Jean Rousset:

We must of course remember that it is a kind of grid constructed by us, the twentieth-century historians, and not by seventeenth-century artists. One

[19] The term seems to have been in use, though with different connotations, as early as the thirteenth century, but it is said that the first person to use it (with capital letters) to mean the whole period between antiquity and the Renaissance was Michelet (according to M. Bloch, *The Historian's Craft* (1954; 1976 edn.), 178–81). However, *OED*, strong on this point, makes it plain that the usage was known in England as early as 1753 (Middle Age) and, as 'Middle Ages', by 1819.

[20] *Renaissance and Renascences*, p. 29.

must avoid confusing the grid and the artists, the interpretative schema and the works undergoing interpretation. The categories are only means of investigating these facts, the works; and one should think of them as working hypotheses, instruments of research, scaffoldings which lose their utility once the building is finished.[21]

But it is very difficult to remember all this when actually using the period words; or when we substitute for them new sets of words and talk about epistèmes or discourse-formations. The last thing you can say about them is that in real use they are 'value-free'; they not only impose valuations on particular works and particular periods, but they all tend more or less silently to place uniquely high value on our own period, since it is on behalf of that period that the valuations are made. We want to select from the past what is modern about it and assume that we have a very privileged view of the past that enables us to do so. In other words, periods are another way of making modern.

It has been said that 'periodization is colonial politics',[22] which makes 'period' as wicked an idea as 'canon'. It is certainly true of both that they are used to serve our interests, which may be colonialist or political. As Karl Popper remarks, 'Although history has no meaning, we can give it a meaning.'[23] He believes that we should choose such meanings, as we should choose our ends in life, which also has no meanings other than those we give it, by an exercise of conscientious reason. This, no doubt, would always be the claim of the chooser. The meanings chosen will necessarily vary. But most agree that it is a benefit to secure access—by '(re)construction', as Jameson might say—to something in the past that can be made new, made valuable for the present. We may recall that Freud gave some thought to the historical validity of 'constructions', maintaining to the end that the contact between the construction and historical reality wasn't delusive.[24]

Let me give an example from the history of poetry: a critic can try to establish the pre-eminence of certain kinds of poetry by means of

---

[21] J. Rousset, 'La Définition du terme "baroque"', in *Actes du IIIe Congrès de l'Association Internationale de Littérature Comparée* (1962), 167, quoted in C. Guillèn *Literature as System* (1971), 428.

[22] Heiner Mueller, quoted in S. Trachtenberg (ed.), *The Postmodern Movement* (1985), 243.

[23] *The Open Society and its Enemies* (1945; 1962 edn.), ii. 278.

[24] 'Constructions in Analysis' (1937), *Standard Edition*, xxiii.

revaluation, and revaluations often take the form of claiming that a certain period has been overvalued while another has been neglected. The old is made new by association or application; it is not only in the present state of culture that the label 'modern' confers value: there was, long ago, a *musica moderna*, a *devotio moderna*. There have been many modern poetries, now a matter for the history books, but all in their time requiring a revaluation of the past. The handiest example is the revaluation of the poetry of Donne. Once read only as a curiosity, well outside the main tradition, he came to be strongly associated with a specifically modern kind of writing; and this connection could be made in very different ways, Francis Thompson's and Eliot's and Empson's for instance. Thompson admired Donne's blend of 'sensoriness' and intellect; Eliot developed this insight and found in Donne an indication of our loss, by historical catastrophe, of the power to think and feel simultaneously; Empson admired what he took to be Donne's involvement in a modern age of science, an involvement closely resembling Empson's in the new science of the early twentieth century.

The next step was to establish retroactively a movement, also a period, by grouping with Donne some essentially very different poets (Herbert, Vaughan, Marvell, Cleveland, etc.) as exponents of 'Metaphysical' poetry. The term was an old one, and in its early use had been dyslogistic, even dismissive; but, like so many others, it was now adopted as an honorific. And the next move was to convert this minor movement into something closer to a megaperiod; Metaphysical was now said to be a subdivision of Baroque, considered as a pan-European period, so that the English poets were associated with European poets which, before the invention of these new criteria, most of them did not much resemble—Góngora in Spain, Marino in Italy[25]—and with particular kinds of music and painting and even politics. Moreover a preference for Donne's kind of poetry could be used as a basis for large generalizations about the course of English history, a process sketched by Eliot and elaborately developed by others.

In all such matters we obey imperatives of various sorts, and

---

[25] It is true that Dr Johnson, in his '*Life of Cowley*' (1779), said that the 'metaphysical' kind of writing 'was, I believe, borrowed from Marino and his followers', but the claim is clearly very tentative and has no obvious relation to the concept of Baroque, which was of course as unknown to Johnson as, in all probability, the poetry of Marino and his followers.

ambitions by no means entirely disinterested; and then we find reasons whereby to impose our new periods and valuations on others. We choose early seventeenth-century poetry for all sorts of reasons—a recurrent desire for splendid or lurid religious sentiment, a conviction that our own poetry is private and witty and wry (Laforgue goes well with Donne, we say, and private, witty, wry poetry of the Laforguian sort we aspire to write has been unaccountably neglected) or even because we suppose that the Civil War ended a state of society we prefer to the one we have. The virtues evident in the arts of the pre-Civil War period are not to be found in later periods, their absence being most marked in the most recent period of all, at least until our arrival on the scene, which justifies their modernity by association with our own.

The reasons we give for choosing periods and authors always change, along with changed valuations. Sixty years ago the propaganda for current changes and preferences was so successful that we now identify that period as Modern (later, Modern*ist*) which of course all periods once were, though none can be henceforth. That is why 'Postmodern' has followed so quickly; and why there is a body of 'canonical' Modern or Modernist works which belong to the past. You aren't required to love these works, but, whether you do or, like Lukács for instance don't, you have no difficulty identifying them by the label. And now we study their interactions like those of other canonical works; they don't change, but we adapt them by interpretation, by new studies of their internal characteristics and of their relations to the intellectual contexts of their own time and ours. So the Modern, which sixty years ago was the criterion for the validity of other periods and canonical choices, is now itself a period, and its works are fully canonical and even subject to attack for being so.

My contention is that the forces which control our treatment of history in general are the same forces which insist that we think in terms of period, and, especially when the documents in question are literary, in terms of canon. That the choices made in all these fields are controlled by the desires of the mind and even by the desire for power I cannot contest, though conscience may also have its part, as Popper would wish.

There is one aspect of the question I haven't sufficiently mentioned, namely that authoritative choices, although conceivably the first motion may come from an individual, normally require a consensus, and the consensus of a relatively small number of people.

In the case of literature we may identify these persons with what Fish calls an 'interpretive community'. There must be institutional control of interpretation, as I've argued at length elsewhere,[26] and self-perpetuating institutions resist not only those they think of as incompetent for reasons of ignorance, but also the charismatic outsider. They are bound to be reactionary in some sense; the young are trained to make certain kinds of interpretation of the favoured texts, they become senior and have themselves an interest in an inherited, if modified, set of procedures, and have to make a large investment in the canon. This does not mean that there are no sects and no discontent within the institution—anybody, today, looking at schools and faculties of literature, can see sectarian discontent. There is always a possibility that within a large and not particularly centralized institution there may develop subcanons and revisions of periodization, to suit, say, feminists and Afro-Americans or Derrideans, or even feminist Afro-American Derrideans. What is certain is that revolutionary revisions would require transfers of powers, a reign of literary terror the prospect of which many of us enjoy less than the Professor of English and Human Relations. And the business of valuing selected moments and selected books, saved from the indiscriminate mass of historical fact, would in any case continue. So would the inherited methods of analysis and evaluation (for example the 'metaphorical patterns that are common to past and present black women writers'). Absolute justice and perfection of conscience are unlikely to be more available under that new dispensation than they are now.

All the same, we do accept change, in the ways we conceive as open to us. But so long as we seek value in works of the past we shall be forced to submit the show of history to the desires of the mind—whoever 'we' may be. And in order to do that we shall invent new grids and impose them on the past—rewrite the past to suit our modern wishes, as the past has always been rewritten. Yet valuations are handed on, and constantly redefined; so that in the end the question is not whether they are unfairly selective, but whether we want to break the only strong link we have with the past—our ability to identify with the interests of our predecessors, to qualify their judgements without necessarily overthrowing them, to converse with them in a transhistorical dimension. Though inevitably

---

[26] Kermode, *Essays on Fiction* (in US *The Art of Telling*) (1983).

tainted with privilege and injustice, that still seems a valuable inheritance; some catastrophe might conceivably destroy it, but the destruction should not be encouraged by members of the rather small community that cares about writing or about art in general. Some workable notion of canon, some examined idea of history, though like most human arrangements they may be represented as unjust and self-serving, are necessary to any concept of past value with the least chance of survival, necessary even to the desired rehabilitation of the unfairly neglected. So the tradition of value, flawed as it is, remains valuable. Certainly it should be constantly scrutinized, so that the past, already diminished by our necessary selective manipulations, is not reduced even further by unnecessary compliance with fashion or prejudice. For we are always under that threat, one form of which I shall look at in the next chapter, when my business with be with the fashions of Postmodernity.

7 · Fragments and Ruins

I BEGIN with another little demonstration of the potential for muddle in the extended use of period descriptions and explanatory historical myths. They can break loose, or be forced into service by some pressure group, or be reduced by ignorance to nonsense. The expression 'dissociation of sensibility' was coined by Rémy de Gourmont, who applied it to the psychology of the poet, but its meaning changed at once when T. S. Eliot borrowed it as a neat modern way of putting an idea already quite ancient, in his essay on the Metaphysical poets (1921). As everybody knows, Eliot said that around the time of the Civil War a dissociation of sensibility set in from which we have never recovered; it became impossible to think and feel simultaneously. There have been endless arguments about the implications, historical and aesthetic, of this insight, and a good deal of scepticism about its validity. Some thought it an attempt to rewrite the history of poetry in the interest of Eliot, who wanted to reorganize the past in such a way that it would support his own poetic practice, about to be revealed in *The Waste Land*.

All that is familiar ground. But lately the term has undergone curious new transformations. For instance, the *Times* obituary of Sonia Delaunay (5 December 1979) records that, with the help of her husband, Mme Delaunay invented Orphism. Orphism is described as a movement 'related to Futurism in its preoccupation with the artistic expression of such specifically twentieth-century phenomena as speed and simultaneity of experience (very much what Eliot defined as dissociation of sensibility)'. Of course there is no connection whatever between the isms here mentioned and Eliot's idea —which in any case had to do with a *loss* of simultaneity. In the same year, 1979, there appeared August Weidmann's book *Romantic Roots in Modern Art*, which has a whole section on dissociation of sensibility. It doesn't even mention Eliot, but describes the phrase as 'currently in vogue', and explains its association with the Expressionist faith in 'primary vision', which is glossed as the intermission of ordinary vision. In identifying 'primary vision' with 'dissociation of sensibility' the author seems to think they both imply something like Rimbaud's derangement of all the senses. As it happens,

Widemann dislikes Expressionism, so dissociation of sensibility, after making this very peculiar journey, ends by being once more a bad thing, as it was for Eliot, but not at all the same bad thing that it was for Eliot.

Once a term of this kind takes off there is no knowing where it will go; there are no societies for the preservation of its original sense or even for the prevention of its nonsensical use. That this is as true of megaperiods as it is of minor inventions like 'dissociation of sensibility', a moment's thought about 'Postmodern' and related terms will show. It is as if these expressions came into being and then had to be given meanings. They are of quite recent origin. The first recorded use of 'Postmodern' in the *OED Supplement* goes back to 1949, but it was used to describe a kind of architecture that came later than, and reacted against, the Modern Movement in that field. This clear and restricted sense is still current and still eulogistic; a writer in *The Times Literary Supplement*, 2 May 1986, says the masters of the Modern Movement 'must now have reached their lowest point', so Postmodern is good and Modern is bad. In a more general sense Arnold Toynbee claimed in 1956 that we had reached the Postmodern Age, an observation ripe for various interpretation. For example, Harry Levin, quoting Toynbee in a lecture given in 1960, took him to mean that we were no longer in the Modern Period of Matthew Arnold; finished for the moment with revolution, we were consolidating the gains of the great Moderns.[1] This is very far from the senses later accumulated.

The first recorded use of the term to characterize a whole movement or a whole period, an epoch in the history of culture and society or of Man, seems to occur in a lecture given by Leslie Fiedler in 1965. He predicted a great widening of the generation gap and the formation of an entirely new culture or counter-culture, with the young using hallucinogens instead of alcohol and the past disappearing from the scene along with Reason.[2] Daniel Bell, in an essay begun in 1969 though first published in 1977, also took a broad sociological look at Postmodernism, which he saw as the victory of an anti-bourgeois culture, of antinomianism and anti-institutionalism, over middle-class values in life and art. Within Modernism there was a party profoundly committed to tradition, or a version of it; there was

---

[1] 'What was Modernism?' in *Refractions* (1966), 271–95.
[2] 'The New Mutants', *Partisan Review* (Fall 1965), 518.

another, an antinomian, past-hating party, the avant-garde of Dada
and Surrealism, and according to Bell it is this movement which has
come to cultural power in Postmodernism. The effort of Postmodernism is 'to erase all boundaries' in the psychic and erotic life as
well as in the arts.[3] Bell, who clearly dislikes the phenomena associated with Postmodernism, simultaneously deplores and dignifies
them by associating them not only with triviality in artistic and social
behaviour but also with large social issues such as the erosion of
legitimacy. In fact he sees the trivia as intimately related to the larger
issues: 'antinomianism exhausts itself in the search for novelty' and
must eventually collapse, its challenges and experiments producing
everdiminishing returns, into anomie.[4]

However, my concern is primarily with the ways in which this
period description is used in the context of literature and the arts.
Malcolm Bradbury and James McFarlane, in their excellent collection *Modernism* of 1976, also wondered whether Postmodernism
wasn't Dada come round again in the form of the counter-culture.
There was some doubt not only about the value of whatever
Postmodernism was, but also about whether it was only something
old in new dress or something radically new, a cultural formation
proper to a universe in which not only God but Man had died, and so
on. There is a good deal of babbling, but the term has clearly come to
stay, and people latch on to it as on to other period descriptions; there
is now a Postmodernist theology.

In search of enlightenment I turned to a recent work called
The Postmodern Moment, and find the editor saying that, whereas
Modernism is closed in form and so needs to be explained by
reference to something outside it, Postmodernism calls for no such
referential explication; it does not symbolize but signify, it is a
presence and not the symbol of an absence. The old Modernists
—those whose works are now included in the 'Modernist canon'
—are dismissed as collaborators with late capitalism and 'the official
culture'; Postmodernism, in contrast, may be seen as 'a guerrilla
action, dislodging the logic of a repressive state'. As for the past, the
response of Postmodernism to the past is not to react against it but to
use it for decorative purposes. And its response to reality is to treat it
as unreal.

[3] 'Beyond Modernism, Beyond Self', in *The Winding Passage* (1980), 275–302.
[4] Ibid., p. xxii.

The fact that it doesn't matter to its exponents whether what they say about it is trivial or false is bound to make life difficult for old-fashioned investigators of Postmodernism. One of the contributors to Trachtenberg's collection tells us that a distinguishing characteristic of the Postmodern period is our sense of living at the end of an epoch—an observation so comprehensively ignorant as to defy polite correction. Another contributor informs us learnedly that nobody had supposed the daguerrotype would replace the painted portrait. If you know anything at all about the subject you know that this was in fact quite a common expectation.[5] This is what happens when you use the past for decorative purposes. These may seem to be small matters, but they are symptomatic, and it isn't surprising that Hilton Kramer thinks of 'Postmodernism' as what happened after the demise of the moral and aesthetic authority of Modernism ('under the new post-modernist dispensation, anything goes'[6]). But this kind of grumbling means nothing to the propagandists of Postmodernism, who, as we have seen, rejoice that they are rid of precisely that authority and need no longer 'collaborate' with an official repressive culture that sets store by truth and the past.

It may seem that there isn't a lot of point in arguing about this; if one were to accuse the Postmodernists of claiming out of ignorance that they were doing something new when they were simply repeating something old, or of rewriting the past as pastiche, they would simply agree; what seems to the complainant a disgrace is to them a grace. The American critic Edward Mendelson is shocked to learn that the National Endowment for the Humanities funds Postmodern art of a trivial and disgusting kind, and concludes that to subvent a tame avant-garde concerned with 'gratuitous gestures, empty "concepts", visions of anomie and helplessness without external cause', with 'lumpen disgruntlement' and 'historical amnesia', suits our masters very well; in other words, the Postmodernists, in spite of their believing the contrary, are also, though unwittingly, collaborators with the system, the victims of what Marcuse used to call repressive desublimation.[7] Approaching the question from a

---

[5] P. Stevick, 'Literature', in S. Trachtenberg (ed.), *The Postmodern Movement* (1985), 135. On the daguerrotype question, see W. Ivins, *Prints and Visual Culture* (1953), and L. Steinberg, *Other Criteria* (1972), 62.

[6] In the *New York Times*, 13 Apr. 1980, quoted by D. Crimp, 'On the Museum's Ruins', in H. Foster, *Postmodern Culture* (1985), 44.

[7] *London Review of Books*, 3–16 Sept. 1981.

quite different political direction, Terry Eagleton associates Post-modernism with commodity fetishism;[8] Marxists have on the whole been suspicious of most Modernisms, fearing 'bourgeois disinte-gration, decay, decadence . . . aimless anarchist revolt'.[9] And it is true that many manifestations of Postmodernism are of the kind Christopher Caudwell described as bourgeois anarchism. But to the enthusiastic Postmodernist, complaints of this kind simply testify to the absurdly bourgeois views of history and society taken by adherents of a largely forgotten nineteenth-century ideology.

In short, Postmodernism is another of those period descriptions that help you to take a view of the past suitable to whatever it is you want to do. It ceases to be attached to a particular historical moment. Instead of coming after Modernism it can be regarded as coeval with it, or even as preceding it. It is now possible to describe Duchamp as an anti-Modernist—which on some views is much the same thing as a Postmodernist—though he used to be naïvely thought of as a Modernist of exceptional importance. Now he is said to have made 'an all-out frontal attack on the aesthetic principles of modernism', just as Rauschenberg did later when he erased a draw-ing of de Kooning's, thus 'marking the nascent drive of a new spirit to cleanse itself from the painterly and critical constraints of modernism'.[10]

Any sound explanation of these muddles—and they may be too trivial to deserve one—would have to be historical, and therefore in principle not available to Postmodernists. A clue to the character of such an explanation may be found in an essay by Paul de Man, written in 1969 and called 'Literary History and Literary Modernity'. De Man remarks that 'literature, which is inconceivable without a passion for modernity, also seems to oppose from the inside a subtle resistance to this passion'. And he goes on:

the continuous appeal of modernity, the desire to break out of literature toward the reality of the moment, prevails, and, in its turn, folding back upon itself, engenders the repetition and continuation of literature. Thus modernity, which is fundamentally a falling away from literature, and a rejection of history, also acts as the principle that gives literature duration and historical existence.

[8] *Against the Grain* (1986), 131–48.
[9] M. Szabolsci, 'Avant-Garde, Neo-Avant-Garde, Modernism: Questions and Suggestions', *New Literary History*, 3 (1971–2), 50.
[10] J. T. Paoletti, 'Art', in Trachtenberg, *Postmodern Movement*, pp. 58, 59.

He further observes that 'a partisan and deliberately pro-Modern [sc. 'postmodern'] stance is much more easily taken by someone devoid of literary sensibility than by a genuine writer'.[11]

In the nature of the case this is a permanent state of affairs; a tension between history and modern value (or between Modern and Postmodern) is constitutive of all literature, so that to suppose the present situation to be unique is simply wrong, and arises from a partisan desire to advertise only half of the truth and in particular to emphasize discontinuity and novelty. Duchamp showed that if you put some ordinary object into a physical or aesthetic context normally appropriated to art, that object acquires some at least of the privilege of objects intended to be works of art. This is now taken to mean that anything is art if you say it is. John Cage greatly enlarged the aleatory element that is present in all art, and we are therefore asked to believe that all art should be random and fragmentary.

This is an important point, for a suspicion of totalities is endemic in Postmodernist thought. There is a tension between whole and fragment analogous to de Man's tension between modernity and history. And I now have to say something about this business of honest fragments and illusory wholes.

Already twenty years ago it was being said that syntactically ordered sentences were Fascist, and I remember asking whether it was thought a good neo-Dadaist and democratic idea to randomize the telephone book. Organized wholes were abhorrent, at best remnants of bourgeois liberalism, at worst images of totalitarian repression. It became necessary to find new value in fragments regarded not as parts of wholes but as ends in themselves, and the truth of human experience, even if that turned out to be a bit of a joke. So began the Postmodern love-affair with the fragment.[12]

---

[11] *Blindness and Insight* (1971), 154, 162.

[12] Since the chapter was written there has appeared an interesting essay by Ihab Hassan, for long an eminent public relations man for Postmodernism. Hassan offers a list of 'eleven traits' of Postmodern literary culture (indeterminacy, decanonization, carnivalization, etc.) and one of these, as you would expect, is 'fragmentation': 'the postmodernist only disconnects; fragments are all he pretends to trust. His worst insult, objurgation, is the word *totalization*, by which he means any synthesis whatever, social, epistemic, poetic . . .' He then discusses the contention between Habermas and Lyotard as 'triangulated' by Richard Rorty in 'Habermas, Lyotard, et la postmodernité', *Critique*, 12 (1986), 503–20, and offers to 'square the triangle', supporting Lyotard's ludicity and rejection of metanarratives, though with quite severe qualifications. ('Making Sense: The Trials of Postmodern Discourse', *New Literary History*, 18 (1987), 437–59.).

We should not be surprised to learn that although very modern the philosophy of the fragment has a long history. It was a pre-occupation of the German Romantics, the modernists of their day. Friedrich Schlegel wrote many fragments about fragments. He is the true ancestor of all who need to care about fragments because they distrust wholes.

Jean-François Lyotard tells us in his influential book *La Condition postmoderne: Rapport sur le savoir* (1977) that 'postmodernism' is 'the state of our culture following the transformations which, since the end of the nineteenth century, have altered the game rules for science, literature and the arts'. Whereas 'modern' legitimates itself with reference to a metadiscourse, 'some grand narrative', 'post-modern' is defined as 'incredulity toward metanarratives'. It deals in 'particles' which are heterogeneous elements in language games, and not in the validating totality of a metalanguage. Consequently knowledge is reduced to marketable 'bits'. Modernist art used its techniques to make visible something beyond or outside it, invisible until so treated. Postmodernism deconstructs such techniques. It denies itself 'the solace of good forms'. It has nothing whatever to do with totalities. It must always be a collection of bits or fragments. Lyotard is glad to see the end of totalities. 'We have paid a high enough price for the nostalgia of the whole and the one. . . . Let us wage war on totality.' The fragment is the symbol of our condition and of our authenticity.[13]

I must omit consideration of the fact that Lyotard's aim is in part polemical, since he is contesting the views of Jürgen Habermas, who favours a return to Modernist rationality.[14] Instead, as a possible aid to understanding, a prophylactic or propaedeutic, I will insert a digression, an interesting page of writing about fragmentariness:

Before reaching Knightsbridge, Mr. Verloc took a turn to the left out of the busy main thoroughfare, uproarious with the traffic of swaying omnibuses and trotting vans, in the almost silent, swift flow of hansoms. Under his hat, worn with a slight backward tilt, his hair had been carefully brushed into respectful sleekness; for his business was with an Embassy. And Mr. Verloc, steady like a rock—a soft kind of rock—marched now along a street which could with every propriety be described as private. In its breadth, emptiness,

[13] *The Postmodernist Condition*, trans. G. Bennington and B. Massumi (1984), pp. xxii ff., 81.
[14] His important essay 'Modernity – An Incomplete Project' is now accessible in H. Foster (ed.), *Postmodern Culture* (1985) 3–15.

and extent it had the majesty of inorganic nature, of matter that never dies. The only reminder of mortality was a doctor's brougham arrested in august solitude close to the curbstone. The polished knockers of the doors gleamed as far as the eye could reach, the clean windows shone with a dark opaque lustre. And all was still. But a milk cart rattled noisily across the distant perspective; a butcher boy, driving with the noble recklessness of a charioteer at Olympic Games, dashed round the corner sitting high above a pair of red wheels. A guilty-looking cat issuing from under the stones ran for a while in front of Mr. Verloc, then dived into another basement; and a thick police constable, looking a stranger to every emotion, as if he, too, were part of inorganic nature, surging apparently out of a lamp-post, took not the slightest notice of Mr. Verloc. With a turn to the left Mr. Verloc pursued his way along a narrow street by the side of a yellow wall which, for some inscrutable reason, had No. 1 Chesham Square written on it in black letters. Chesham Square was at least sixty yards away, and Mr. Verloc, cosmopolitan enough not to be deceived by London's topographical mysteries, held on steadily without a sign of surprise or indignation. At last, with business-like persistency, he reached the Square, and made diagonally for number 10. This belonged to an imposing carriage gate in a high, clean wall between two houses, of which one rationally enough bore the number 9 and the other was numbered 37; but the fact that this last belonged to Porthill Street, a street well known in the neighbourhood, was proclaimed by an inscription placed above the ground-floor windows by whatever highly efficient authority is charged with the duty of keeping track of London's strayed houses.

That passage is from Conrad's *The Secret Agent*, published in 1907. Some say human nature changed in 1905, some in 1910, so 1907 is a fair median. But the idea of the city as full of flashing discontinuities, irrational intrusions, bewildering fragments, absurd juxtapositions, was far from new even in 1907. The discovery or rediscovery of Bakhtin has lately given wider currency to the idea of the carnavalesque, and we should hardly hesitate to assign this passage of Conrad's to that mode. Walter Benjamin's essay on Baudelaire is a striking comment on it as it existed half a century earlier. We are in everyday life so familiar with the phenomenon—the carnavalesque city—that we should hardly attend to it if our attention were not compelled by works of art, or by comment so shrewd that it operates like a work of art, to subvert habit and defamiliarize the scene. We ordinarily know how to make wholes of fragments; we do it in the cinema and walking around the city. When Benjamin speaks of the city as a series of discontinuous shocks or shots, moments of 'switching, inserting, pressing, snapping', of aimless glances, of alternations between isolation and collision, we know exactly what he means, and we agree that it takes an artist–*flâneur* to register the barrage of impressions we get from dealing with objects that do not return our glance and yet not neglect what he calls aura—the very quality that mechanical reproduction destroys, the quality that requires the transposition of the response common in human relationships to our relations with inanimate objects, so that they present us with the past they have absorbed, offer us something different from mere things, as the last book of Proust transforms the memories scattered about the earlier ones.[15]

Benjamin believed that aura owed its existence to capitalist oppression, but also that it stood for an essential wholeness, for the correspondences between parts or fragments that make the integrity of a world. The tension between these beliefs gives his criticism a tragic note; yet it is carnavalesque, and he had what George Steiner calls a penchant for 'arcane tomfoolery'[16]—a touch of *blague* that was a recurring feature in the art of the time, a carnavalesque air appropriate to the fragmented city. It is worth recalling that histories of Dada associate its successive epochs with the names of cities, progressively more metropolitan, more fragmented, more difficult to hold in a single thought: Zurich, Paris, New York.

In Conrad's novel London is the world metropolis, and the bomb plot against Greenwich Observatory is an attempt on the heart of the world and the wholeness of the world. In the closing pages the anarchist professor walks the streets with a lethal bomb in his pocket, prepared to blow any challenger, and himself, into fragments; and this is how he would deal, if he could—a booby-trapped Lyotard —with the man-made order or master-narrative of the world or of London, its chosen centre. For London, though it may be perceived as fragments, is essential to the idea of the wholeness of the world. Zero longitude runs through its heart; the lines of longitude may be as lacking in relation to reality as the circles drawn by the half-witted boy Stevie, but they are required for the commerce and communications of a world centred on London. The totality of London (or of the world) is not necessarily a beautiful or admirable totality; the heart of the world is dark, Whitehall is a mere ditch running through its

---

[15] W. Benjamin, *Illuminations* (1968), 157 ff.
[16] Introduction to W. Benjamin, *The Origin of German Tragic Drama* (1977), 1–24.

darkness; yet a totality it is. But fragmentariness is also of its essence; it is a whole made up of a million randomnesses, sometimes horrible, like the scattered parts of the boy Stevie, but sometimes eerily facetious, full of *blague*, the neighbouring mode into which ironists habitually fall.

The passage I quoted describes Mr Verloc, the minor double agent, on his way to an appointment with the foreign diplomat who pays him. He wants Verloc, as *agent provocateur*, to stir up some useful terrorism. The interview is itself wonderfully grotesque, but its tone is prepared by this passage describing Verloc's approach to the embassy. Bakhtin remarks that

all the images of carnival are dualistic; they unite within themselves both poles of change and crisis, birth and death (the image of pregnant death), blessing and curse, praise and abuse, youth and old age, top and bottom, face and backside, stupidity and wisdom. Very characteristic of carnival thinking are paired images, chosen for their contrast (high/low, fat/thin, etc.) or for their similarity (doubles, twins) . . .[17]

Verloc's London is as carnivalized as Dostoevsky's St Petersburg. It is at once uproarious and quiet, trotting and flowing, wide and narrow. Mr Verloc's fatness is that of a soft rock; a thin lamp-post spawns a fat policeman; inorganic nature gives birth to a cat; solid houses appear to have wandered from their sites, and the sequence of their numbers is thrown into confusion. Immortal matter is contiguous with the doctor's brougham, emblem of mortality. Knockers gleam brightly, windows darkly. The policeman and Verloc, alike instruments of order, and twinned in obesity, ignore each other; they register no emotion, though the cat looks guilty. They meet in a public street that is nevertheless private. You might say the whole passage is in direct descent from the Belsey Bob passages in the Mummers' Plays; or, better, from an ancient tradition of carnival now newly assimilated to the genre of the novel; and perhaps not so newly, since it had been at home there for a long time before Conrad so deliberately heightened it.

Later the association of Verloc and the policeman is reaffirmed when the freak voice of the former summons the latter in the park. And, like the collection of revolutionaries in the book, who are also

---

[17] M. Bakhtin, *Problems of Dostoevsky's Poetics* (1984), 126. On the carnivalization of the city in Dostoevsky, see pp. 160 ff.

fat, Verloc and the policeman are pregnant with death. We remember these collocated disparities along with the crazy cabhorse staggering across London, the monstrous mechanical piano in the absurdly decorated beerhall; like the professor we caress 'images of ruin and destruction', fragmentation, chaos, while at the same time seeing that, also like his professor, Conrad holds this world together by means of an artefact, compact but explosive, not a bomb but a book—single, yet compounded of opposites, contradictions, and false concords: so that a world blown to pieces, to be looked at awry and in no other way, may rightly be seen as, for a moment, rich in correspondence, a momentary *civitas*. Carnival is a licensed and temporary disorder, but the order from which it is a vacation is no longer that of a world or a society, to be restored by a change in the seasons or in the liturgical calendar. It is not to be restored except in the perceived order of a book.

Conrad himself is holding together the complementary and antithetical ideas of wholeness and fragmentation. When he speaks of fragments he might almost have been making the city ready for the Dada carnival a decade later. Dada is interested *only* in fragments. Programmatically anarchic and fragmentary, Dada is meant to be the equivalent in art of the professor's bomb in the street full of men. Disowning the past it disowns totality and aura and disowns any desire to achieve a Benjaminite, Proustian, or Conradian recovery of it. It is dispersion, babble, unrelated happenings, shock, *blague*, arcane tomfoolery, carnival cries. It condemns to death the past and its agreements about form and wholeness, but it does so with a deliberately irresponsible gaiety and a measure of self-irony. It is full of contradictions: absolutely new, absolutely unconstrained, it nevertheless owes much to Cubism. Futurism, and Expressionism. Its death sentences were framed earlier by Marinetti. Werner Haftmann tells us that the photomontages of Haussmann were developed from a Futurist technique and were intended 'to produce an all-embracing dynamic pattern of interpenetrating aspects of reality—a system in short, a universe of correspondence. Yet Haftmann also says that Dada succeeded in cutting 'the umbilical cord that bound us to history' simply because it refused to see itself as so bound.[18]

---

[18] W. Haftmann, Postscript to Hans Richter, *Dada: Art and Anti-art*, trans. D. Britt (1965), 215–22.

Here we have the contradiction or tension that haunts the philosophy of the fragment. Proust spoke in a letter of 'a kind of blending
into a transparent unity, in which all things, losing their first
appearance as things, come together and arrange themselves in a sort
of order, bathed in the same light, seen in terms of each other,
without a single word that resists this assimilation and stays outside
the pattern . . .'[19] And Gilles Deleuze, commenting rather uneasily
on the problem of totalization in Proust, writes:

We have given up seeking a unity which would unify the parts, a whole which
would totalize the fragments. For it is the character and nature of the parts or
fragments to exclude the Logos both as logical unity and as organic totality.
But there is, there must be a unity which is the unity *of* this very multi-
plicity, a whole which is the whole *of* just these fragments: a One and a
Whole which . . . would function as effect, effect of machines, instead of as
principles. A communication which would not be posited as a principle, but
which would result from the operation of the machines and their detached
parts, their noncommunicating fragments.[20]

Here the attempt is to evade the old organicism by substituting a
totality of mechanical fragments, on the analogy of a car or an
aeroplane.

So we can reasonably say that over the philosophy or propaganda
of the fragment there broods inescapably the shadow of totality. We
come now to the most elaborate and philosophical modern medita-
tion on fragments known to me, which is Maurice Blanchot's book
L'Écriture du désastre. It is no doubt possible to think about fragments
in an unfragmented way—indeed we shall shortly see that it is—but
Blanchot prefers to meditate fragmentarily, on several topics including fragments, in a series of *pensées*. The passages on fragments
surface from time to time in the fragmentary progress of the work,
affected obscurely by their varying contexts, fragments among
fragments, sometimes sibylline and always dark. I may be accused of
the error of trying to read this example of late Romantic irony in an
unironical way, in my search for some tediously univocal truth; and I
have to admit that my accusers might be right.

Fragments, we are told, are not necessarily related to the fragmentary; indeed a fragment so related would indicate 'the end at last',

---

[19] Quoted and translated by J. M. Cocking in *Proust: Collected Essays on the Writer
and his Art* (1982), 252.
[20] *Proust and Signs* (1972), 144-5.

whereas every fragment, 'though unique, repeats, and is undone by repetition'. This seems to mean that repetition destroys the fragmentariness of the fragment by relating it to something else, namely its own repetition, so beginning a pattern. On the other hand there is a point at which knowledge becomes 'finer and lighter' because it does not 'submit' to truth, and 'the non-true, which is not falsehood [and so presumably is fictive] draws knowledge outside the system into the space . . . where repetition does not serve meaning'. So, in spite of what we were told earlier about them, even repeated fragments can evade assimilation by repetition. In the space it enters the fragment need not submit to the system; it remains an independent form of knowledge even if repeated. Thus it appears that the fragment has two modes of existence, ambiguously in and out of the true, in and out of the non-true, *in* the system yet still independent of it. Here is one of those dilemmas or aporiai which it is the peculiar if perverse delight of modern criticism to discover; the inexpressible comfort of intellectual discomfort.

Blanchot, however, feels some obscure wish to move away from that sharp point, if only on to another painful position, and does so by launching a series of negations: the fragment is without external limit, without internal limitation. 'No fullness, no void.' In so far as its world has neither space nor time it allows, as the rabbis said of the Torah, no distinction between late and early, ahead and behind. Fragments connote insufficiency and disappointment, an absence of totality. But they are never merely 'fallen utterances', and are never immune to elaboration. And now we approach a more positive formulation of the doubleness of the fragment. It can never be alone, and always suggests the possibility of wholeness. 'The fragmentary imperative signals to the System which it dismisses . . . and also ceaselessly invokes.' 'Fragmentation, the mark of a coherence all the firmer in that it has to come undone in order to be reached . . . the pulling to pieces . . . of that which has never pre-existed (really or ideally) as a whole. . . . It can never be reassembled in any future presence.' It dissolves a presupposed totality, though it also suggests that totality even as it acknowledges its impossibility. It ironically proposes a system and simultaneously dissolves it. Without the *idea* of systematic totality there can be no fragment, though the fragment ironizes the system and dismisses its author. And Blanchot finds in Friedrich Schlegel an epigram which expresses the antinomy with desperate exactness: 'To have a system, that is what is fatal for the mind; not to have one, this too is fatal. Whence the necessity to observe, while abandoning, the two requirements at once.'[21] I think no Postmodernist has put the matter more pointedly.

We emerge, perhaps slightly stunned, from these lucubrations (simplified and ordered and probably falsified in my account of them, for they are of course not intended to clear our minds) with an illicit straw or two to clutch at. One can try to think of the fragment as existing absolutely, outside any system or community of thought—as a negativity, a fiction of the knowledge of the non-true. But the effort to do so cannot help affirming a perhaps delusive coherence and totality. To hold both aspects in a single thought is, as Schlegel suggests, both fatal and necessary.

Let us hold on to Blanchot while considering another and rather more robust writer on fragments, who doesn't mind yielding to the tempting rigour of order and finds system useful. This is Roger Shattuck. He starts by discussing the pebble in Sartre's *La Nausée*. This pebble is an 'absolute fragment' because by definition it cannot belong to any larger order of things. 'It is a nauseating fissure or vortex in the real through which the universe will leak out.' It is a negative. (I'm not sure this example really works; such a pebble already has a relation to the universe. But then it is admittedly hard to imagine this 'absolute fragment'.) The next kind of fragment is the 'implicate fragment', which has a positive relation to a system. Examples: the archaeologist's potsherd. Cuvier's single bone, a piece of the True Cross. Such fragments testify to order, to a universe containing correspondences, like those of Swedenborg or Blake (or the Bible, or certain novels). But there is a third kind of fragment, the 'ambiguous', which, to the confusion of our reason, is at once absolute *and* implicate. We recognize this as close to Blanchot's fragment. Either because it is really so or because it suits Shattuck's interest to say so, this kind of fragment is more modern than the other two. He identifies it with the objects in a Cubist painting, in which 'the lines and planes . . . both isolate and connect the everyday motifs they manipulate'.[22]

In other words, there is something about the fragment that both isolates and connects—Shattuck's 'ambiguous' fragment—that suggests the modern, suggests, in fact, that in all this talk of fragments

---

[21] M. Blanchot, *The Writing of the Disaster*, trans. A. Smock (1986), 42, 58, 60, 61.
[22] R. Shattuck, *The Innocent Eye* (1984), 37–9.

we have really been discussing something perfectly familiar. There are totalities and they can be treated as privileged—like the Bible, or like *The Waste Land*. There are totalities and they can be despised, or made ironic, or simply used as the background against which the amusing or the insolent fragment is foregrounded, recommended as the leak through which the old systematic universes are voided. It is a question of interest, of the kind of attention offered. It was well known to the early Modernists that they risked the fate of Balzac's painter in 'Le Chef-d'œuvre inconnu' when the quest for a uniquely elaborate and systematic organization of the picture destroyed it, reduced it to a mess of fragments, including one perfectly painted foot. Yeats thought Pound's *Cantos* ran this risk and repeated the error of Balzac's deluded painter. For those totalitarian Modernists worshipped wholes, provided that they were unprecedented in their forms; they wanted to hold more and more disparate material in a single thought or form. Postmodernists sometimes say that Postmodernism began with the *Cantos*, agreeing that the form had burst and spilled its contents, but applauding, not deploring this accident. It is the deconstruction or destruction of formal constructs that is admired. That perfect foot is for Modernists an image of disaster, for Postmodernists a carnavalesque curiosity. Both sides would agree that it delivers a hefty kick to system.

A passion for fragments tempts one into psychoanalysis. Objects, part–objects; the envious spoiling of the object, its fragmentation in infantile fantasy, and consequent reparation; absolute fragments as paranoid–schizoid, implicate fragments as depressive. But it also invites *blague*, the developed relation between art and jokes or put-ons, and, while one could argue that an excessive addiction to *blague* is regressive, it is of more immediate interest that it commonly depends for its effect on the ambiguity of the fragment. From the time of Dada, the time of Jarry and 'Pataphysics', and indeed from much earlier times, *blague* has been a serious issue in art. It deserves its own history.[23] Obviously it isn't possible unless there is already a concept in place to tease. The absolute fragment is a tease, more or less invented in its modern form when millions of people were being fragmented, warmed therefore by a rather desperate gaiety that was

---

[23] This would have to start at least as early as Friedrich Schlegel; for a shorter view see my 'Objects, Jokes and Art', in *Continuities* (1968), 10–27.

founded on the disparity between the world as officially presented and the facts of the battlefields.

However, it has survived that occasion, and the Postmodern is the continuation of its carnival. But the same difficulty arises; without routine, without inherited structures, carnival loses its point; without social totalities there are no anti-social fragments. You can defy the usual and the routine; you can do as Tzara wished, and read to your audience a paragraph from the evening paper, calling it a poem. But they will not know what you are doing unless they know what a poem usually is, providing a whole of knowledge for your teasing fragment. So with Duchamp's snow shovel and bicycle wheel. They are mechanical fragments but in a designated aesthetic space they are perceived as parts of that whole before they can register themselves as alien to it. Otherwise they would not be jokes or ironies calculated to expose the arbitrariness or tedium of our non-joking normalities. Surrealists were good at doing that, as for example when Picabia's cover design for the periodical *Littérature* split the title into 'Lits et ratures' to demonstrate that wholes to which we are accustomed can have unexpected fragmentary parts.[24] It is from devices of this kind that Lacan inherits his ludic puns, which are deliberately carnavalesque and, if you like, paranoid–schizoid and wilfully regressive.

The paradox of unity in dispersity (which exercised Virginia Woolf so fruitfully in *Between the Acts*, not yet to my knowledge claimed for the Postmodernist de-canon) can't be resolved by a simple decision to disregard unity. That it can't be resolved is a Postmodernist fantasy or myth. The naming of a period, or if I can call it so the -isming of a period, always entails the construction of such a myth, which simplifies history and makes valuation of the work of one period easier by devaluing another period (usually the one that comes immediately before, in this case Modernism).

A recent book by C. K. Stead distinguishes between two kinds of fragment, one 'understood in its particularity' (Pound : good) and the other a mere 'offcut' (Eliot : bad).[25] How does one decide whether a fragment is an offcut or an understandable particularity? It seems to depend on how one feels about the poet in question. Eliot we may dislike because he admired Maurras and in certain ways

---

[24] P. Waldberg, *Surrealism* (1965), 31 (reproduces the cover).
[25] C. K. Stead, *Pound, Yeats, Eliot and the Modernist Movement* (1986), 217, 243. For a fuller discussion see *London Review of Books*, 22 May 1986.

opened himself to the charge of anti-Semitism; Pound, despite his politics and his unquestioned and virulent anti-Semitism, we can admire because with all his foibles he strikes us as an independent spirit. If this is the line we take we can go on to say that, in the case of Eliot, fragments (except in *The Waste Land*) are absolute, whereas Pound's, though they sometimes look absolute, are also implicate, and so achieve a satisfying ambiguity that will not trouble the sympathetic reader. What decides is the quality of one's attention and the character of one's prejudice.

Here we have a simple illustration of the way a period description can be used to give apparent objectivity to opinions and discriminations. Modern fragments in a poet you like are Modernist, in a poet you don't like merely modern. In one case you require the parts to be related to some conceptual or imaginative scheme, in the other you don't. Not to care whether a fragment has any connection with what precedes or follows is a critical programme some would identify with Postmodernism, and it is not surprising that, as I have already remarked, the *Cantos* are sometimes taken to be the juncture between Modernism and Postmodernism.

It has been suggested that the cult of the Postmodern grew up in the academy, nourished by the wish or need to find something new to say; and it is true that the academy has become conscious of the built-in obsolescence of its procedures. It will not be very surprising if we shortly find ourselves in need of a new period to go with new modes of exposition and valuation. Possibly the carnival is coming to an end; possibly not. It may be that literary theory, which has so tight a grip on the institution at the moment, is providing the conceptual whole to which all the fragments can be related without surrendering their status as fragments. Totalities can be occult as well as obvious.

Perhaps, as Schlegel remarked, it is equally fatal to the mind to insist on absoluteness and on implicatedness. But we do it all the time. Steven Weinberg says that, although the parts of the world have become inconceivably small, physicists still intend to discover general laws underlying the whole of nature.[26] Deconstruction would be unlearnable were it not implicated in the whole history of philosophy. It is not so long since Northrop Frye impressed us all by inventing a totalizing physics of literature. And in some form or

---

[26] In a speech delivered in 1985 at Mishkenot Sha'ananim, Jerusalem.

other the desire and pursuit of the whole inevitably continues everywhere, even among those who try to tell us the whole truth about Postmodernist fragments. 'For not in nothing nor in things | Extreme and scattering bright can love inhere,' as Donne, the great poet of nothingness, remarked.

It is because we cannot in the end deal with mere offcuts that we treat history as we do. It is an imaginary whole and we invent fictive parts. Our treatment of it may be a bit rough and ready, but at its best it is at least sensible, and in any case life would be impossible without it. It enables us, individually or in institutions, to have some fairly coherent if unstated views on what is valuable enough to merit our attention and the attention of the generation with whose instruction we are charged.

And judgement of the value of the parts will always depend on a valued whole, for instance a canon. As Dr Johnson observed in his Shakespeare Preface, you cannot call a building high if there are no other buildings: 'Of the first building that was raised, it might be with certainty determined whether it was round or square, but whether it was spacious or lofty must have been referred to time.' Some sort of canon, however variable, makes such determinations possible in literature. It may not be, on some God's-eye view, wholly just; if it is a good thing it is only humanly so. Just as there is a permanent tension between our perceptions of totality and our perceptions of dispersity, so there is between our habit of forgetting and our preservation of archives to facilitate remembering; that is why apocrypha can be revived and accorded something like canonical attention. But on the whole we accept the necessity of neglect, and of fashions in neglect, as the price of ensuring that there may be some values reasonably proof against them.

This doesn't mean that value is dictated entirely by academic choices. To say of a work of art that

> It holds his estimate and dignity
> As well wherein 'tis precious of itself
> As in the prizer —

seems to be possible to all parties. This is so whether one thinks of it as offering a significant presence or a significant absence, an immanent value or a value dependent on its transactions with an ideological context, as some Marxists believe. But there is no magic by which immanent value ensures survival; that depends on our ability so to construct history that the valued object stands out from the unvalued and belongs to a totality of literature rather than to an archive of hopelessly diverse documents. Perhaps the best image for the way we endow with value this and not that memory is Proust's novel: out of the indeterminate, disject facts of history, a core of canonical memory; out of history, value.

INDEX

Aaron, Daniel, *Writers on the Left*, 37n
Ackerley, J. R., 26–7; *My Father and Myself*, 26; *My Sister and Myself*, 27
Acton, Lord, 112
Adam Smith, Janet, 75
Adorno, Theodor, 85, 100
Agate, James, 13
Allott, Kenneth, 49–50; *Collected Poems*, 49
Althusser, Louis, 99
Ambrose, St., 12
Anand, Mulk Raj, 96
Annan, Noel, 25
Appel, Alfred, Jr., *The Annotated Lolita*, 17n
Arlen, Michael, 37
Arnold, Matthew, 129
Ashcroft, Peggy, 13
Ariosto, Ludovico, 119
Auden, W. H., 25, 34, 37, 39, 51, 57–59, 62, 65, 69, 70, 72, 80, 81, 104; 'Out on the lawn', 20; 'O Love, the interest itself', 21, 73–7; *Forewords and Afterwords*, 26–7; *The Dog Beneath the Skin*, 29, 31, 76; *Spain 1937*, 33, 77–80; *Another Time*, 32; 'Heavy Date' (*Collected Poems*, 205–8), 32; 'Here on the cropped grass', 42, 48; 'Certainly our city,' 50; *New Year Letter*, 53; 'Just as his dream foretold' (*The English Auden*, 148), 58; 'Letter to Lord Byron', 59; 'Paid on Both Sides,' (*The English Auden*, 1), 63; *The Orators*, 65; 'It's farewell to the drawing-room's civilized cry', 66–7; 'September 1, 1939', 71, 78; *Look, Stranger!* (*On This Island*), 73; 'In Praise of Limestone' (*Collected Poems*, 414–15), 76; 'Hammerfest', 77; 'Plains', 77

Bagehot, Walter, 45
Bakhtin, Mikhail, 135, 137; *Problems in Dostoevsky's Poetics*, 137n
Balzac, Honoré de, 53, 96, 98, 103, 121; *Séraphîta*, 31; *Sarrasine*, 31; 'Le Chef-d'oeuvre inconnu', 142
Bann, Stephen, 109; *The Clothing of Clio*, 109–10
Barker, George, 48
Barthes, Roland, *Sade, Fourier, Loyola*, 31
Bates, Ralph, 38, 95, 96
Baudelaire, Charles, 58, 59, 120, 135
Bell, Daniel, 'Beyond Modernism, Beyond Self', 129–30
Bell, Julian, 95
Benjamin, Walter, 36; 'The Work of Art in the Age of Mechanical Reproduction' (*Illuminations*, 219–54), 95, 104; 'Theses on the Philosophy of History', 117; 'On Some Motifs in Baudelaire', 135; *The Origin of the Tragic Drama*, 136n

Bennett, Tony, *Formalism and Marxism*, 101
Benveniste, Émile, *Problèmes de linguistique générale*, 19n
Bergonzi, Bernard, *Reading the Thirties*, 24
Blake, William, 14
Blanchot, Maurice, *L'écriture de désastre*, 139–41
Bland, Rosamund, *The Man in the Stone House*, vii
Bloch, *The Historian's Craft*, 122
Blunt, Anthony, 64, 65, 66
Blunt, Wilfrid, 14
Bowen, Elizabeth, *The Death of the Heart*, 65–6
Bradbury, Malcolm, 16; *Modernism*, 130
Brenan, Gerald, 29; *A Life of One's Own*, *Personal Record*, 29n
Brierley, Walter, 35, 95; *The Means Test Man*, 35
Bronzino, Agnolo, 120
Broun, Heywood, 85
Brown, Alec, 94, 97
Browne, Sir Thomas, 120
Bunyan, John, 121
Burckhardt, Jacob, *The Civilization of the Renaissance in Italy*, 119
Burgess, Anthony, 3
Burgess, Guy, 64, 65
Busst, A. J. L., 'The Image of the Androgyne', 31

Cage, John, 133
Caird, Edward, 118
Calder-Marshall, Arthur, *Dead Centre*, 22–3; *Pie in the Sky*, 24, 38; *The Changing Scene*, 37–8
Calderón, Pedro, 120n
Carter, J. L., *The Nymphet*, 16
Caudwell, Christopher, 37, 52, 53, 81, 96, 132; *Illusion and Reality*, 38–41; *Romance and Realism*, 39; *Studies in a Dying Culture*, 40
Ceadel, Martin, 'Popular Fiction and the Next War', 68
Christie, Dame Agatha, *The Secret Adversary*, 105–7
Cleveland, John, 124
Cockburn, Claud, 26
Cocking, J. M., *Proust*, 139n
Collett, Anthony, *The Changing Face of England*, 74–6
Collingwood, R. G., *The Idea of History*, 109n
Collins, William, 120
Connolly, Cyril, 4, 72; *Enemies of Promise*, 23
Conrad, Joseph, 103; *Lord Jim*, 102; *The Secret Agent*, 134–8
Corneille, Pierre, 120n
Craig, David, *The Real Foundations*, 44

Breinigsville, PA USA
05 January 2011
252680BV00002B/55/A